BEADS TO BUCKSKINS

BY
PEGGY SUE HENRY

Beading with stone cabochon and beads is extensively covered in this volume. We show time saving techniques, eight pages full color photographs, plus eight pages of all new color patterns. From cowboy hat earrings to exquisitely styled jewelry; illustrated with written instructions.

MARANATHA

"AMEN"

Matthew 6:33
Seek ye first the kingdom of GOD and his righteousness, and all these things shall be added unto you.

Contents

Introduction

We are pleased to introduce you to a unique and innovative style of beading. Gem stones have always radiated an air of elegance. Their delicate colors and depth of beauty, enchants even the novice.

The use of stone cabochon with glass seed beads has been briefly exposed in Volumes Two through Eight. However, in this volume we cover in depth, how to use stone cabochon and stone beads along with glass beads to create a definitive, magnificent wardrobe of jewelry. Each enchanting piece created exhibits superb taste to that individual and becomes a "one of a kind" rarity to cherish.

Precious stones are a luxury item that few people can afford to use in beadwork. However, the semi-precious stone beads and cabochon are abundant these days and quite affordable. Don't let the words "semi-precious" lead you to believe that these stones are not beautiful. The color photograph section in this volume shows how lovely they can be arranged into an outstanding piece of jewelry.

The more common stones used for these beads are agate, jasper, quartz crystal, onyx, and pearl. Just to give you an idea of the many stones that are available, I will name a few specifically: Amethyst, Amazonite, Adventurine, Black Onyx, Bloodstone, Blue Lace Agate, Carnelian, Dolomite Fluoride, Garnet, Goldstone, Hematite, Howlite (white), Jade, Leopard Skin Jasper, Picture Jasper, Lapis (blue), Malachite, Mother of Pearl, Freshwater Pearls, Quartz Crystal (clear and smoky), Rodonite, Rose Quartz, Smoky Quartz, Sodalite, Crazy Lace, Tiger Eye (gold), Red Tiger Eye, Blue Tiger Eye, Turquoise, Unakite, Montana Moss Agate.

There are many more. However, to name them all such as the Moss Agate and Paua Shell and Coral's would take more pages than we have room.

Most of the stones mentioned above can be purchased in the form of cabochon, round or faceted beads in assorted sizes and shapes. The carved heart and leaf shapes are available in most of the stones mentioned and are very popular. The smallest size beads made in semi-precious stones are two millimeter. In comparison to the tiny glass seed beads used in most beadwork, they seem very large. However, when used as trim beads on a neckline or incorporated with fringe, they compliment the piece and the beadwork automatically takes on the appearance of expensive. The two millimeter stone beads can be used to surround the stone cabochon in a frame of elegance while the glass seed beads are used to form a pattern around the stone beads. In unison combinations of color and design, a distinguished array of beautiful jewelry emerges.

Cabochon and stone beads have been around as long or perhaps longer then glass beads. Now that they are being used so successfully with glass, many people do not know where to buy them. A trip to your local rock shop can be very enlightening. A true "Rock Hound" is usually very pleased to share his or her knowledge with you and can point out many helpful things to look for when buying stone beads.

The popularity of stone beads used in conjunction with glass beadwork has created a new line of inventory for bead and craft stores that are beginning to stock the stones and drilled stone chips.

For the person who really enjoys shopping and looking at literally hundreds and hundreds of pounds of stone beads and cabochon of many colors and sizes, I suggest you attend the Gem and Mineral Shows that are held each fall in Denver, Colorado. The display of beads will overwhelm you and the choices are staggering to the imagination.

At this point, I should explain to you a few differences and points to look for when buying stone beads. One of the most disappointing moments you can experience with some stone beads is to discover the color is not as radiant as you remove them from the original string. Usually, the original string is much brighter and darker in color than the stone bead. Many of the stones are semi-transparent, therefore the string adds color to the stone. So always keep in mind that most stone beads (if at all transparent) will not be as colorful off the string. This problem can be overcome by using the same color thread as the original string while doing your beadwork.

There will be a number of stone beads that are color enhanced or dyed to give the appearance of different stones. I know what you are thinking, "how do you dye a stone?" Believe me, there are ways. This process does not mean it's a bad bead. It just gives you a better selection of colors to choose from in stone beads. A point to remember: "Never display the dyed or color enhanced stone beads in direct sunlight for long periods of time, perhaps hours. They will loose color and sometimes fade completely." Sunlight also effects glass beads.

Don't be discouraged about what you have discovered in this introduction about stone beads. Even though they have a few imperfections, it is well worth exploring the possibilities of higher achievements in beadwork reached by using the stones. It has been the experience of this author, that incorporating stone beads and cabochon to my line of jewelry has opened up new avenues of market. Glass beadwork is classified sometimes to certain styles and therefore is contained in a limited category of stores. Primarily bead stores, trading posts, craft shows, flea markets and individual sales, etc. By adding semi-precious stones I have automatically opened up a market to jewelry companies across the country. You can capitalize on a new design of glass and stone jewelry also.

There is a newly formed bead society in the Denver area, " **The Rocky Mountain Bead Society", 2582 Arapahoe Avenue, Boulder, CO 80302.** The members are very busy arranging their annual Bead Bazaar. However, as a member myself, I can assure you these people will be happy to assist you in anyway they can with information concerning membership or any other functions pertaining to beads in their area.

Acknowledgments

There are so many special people I would like to acknowledge and thank for their contribution to this series of publications. First of all my husband "Richard Henry", who is also my publisher and has put up with me through out the years of research. Allowing me the necessary time to complete beading projects and sponsoring my photography expenses, including new camera equipment and a thousand other little things to numerous to mention. His patience is a gift from God, I'm sure.

To all the talented beaders and crafters that have shared their accomplishments with us and allowed their work to be photographed and exposed in this volume a very special thank you. My heart goes out to all of you for you input and support.

Frieda Bates, Shalimar Tracy, Melody Abbott, Judy Otero, Jennifer Tallbear, Doris Barnes, Toni Acedo, Suzanne Myer, Tamera Dickerson, Ella Johnson, Susan Cochran, Margo Fields, Sheri Nelson, Michelle Wetzel, Deb Horak, William Tohee, Lela Holcomb, Richard Howe, my mother "Heneretta Bedonie", and my dear friend, Russell Daud.

The front cover cabochon beadwork was designed and created by the Author.

All patterns and illustrations were created by the Author with the exception of the clip art "Southwestern Applique page, whish is furnished through the Santa Fe collection; Clip Art @ 1990-1992 RT Computer Graphics.

Most of the Photographers of photos contributed for this and other volumes are unknown to the Author, however I would like to thank all of them, wherever they may be. Many of the beaders do their own photography. The front and back cover of all volumes have been photographed by the Author.

There is a special group of people at Johnson Printing, Boulder, Co., that I would like to acknowledge and thank for all their help and guidance in leading me through this volume. Ann Curtis and Phil Emery have worked with me through the last seven volumes and I have to say "A BIG THANK YOU". It would have been very difficult without you.

A special thanks also to Allen Graves of Portland OR., Unicorn Beading Supply Co. for the use of his rosette graph template and Size-O-Matic bead sizer.

About the Author

It is the desire of this author to preserve and pass on, the techniques for beading used by my family for generations.

In this series are those techniques and other presentations dealing with the Native American Indian. The construction of garments, styles and culture from past to present are addressed. I try to cover as many subjects as possible concerning these issues.

As an admirer of all types of beadwork and crafts from other cultures around the world, I have included European and old world techniques, as well as African, Oriental and South American styles. When it comes to origin of a certain technique of beadwork, it becomes very difficult to say that any particular culture was first to use it. I'm pleased these techniques were developed and passed on regardless of the origin.

Beadwork and other home crafts are very rewarding. I quote Mr. Rufus Coomer, "Take time and perfect your craft to an art form; only then will it become solely yours. When you can develop a style that is yours alone, the demand for your craft will be there". I agree with Mr. Coomer. I also believe that everybody who desires to create can develop their own craft. It begins by setting a goal and working toward that goal with patience as you proceed.

There is a certain mysterious feeling that seems to over take me while doing beadwork. The feeling that I want to do more and I can't seem to lay the project down until I'm finished or just to tired to go on. I have often referred to this feeling as "bead fever". I'm sure that any one who has ever beaded or worked needle craft has experienced this feeling. Enthusiasm of wanting to see what the finished piece will look like continues to hold my interest through out the whole project.

After the piece is finished I get a gratifying feeling of accomplishment. For these reasons alone, I encourage you to take up beading or any other craft you can fill your spare time with. You will find as much pleasure as I have, I'm sure.

Since beginning this series of books; first volume written in 1987 and published in 1988; there has been many other beaders publish their ideas and techniques on the subject of beading. All of whom have very much to offer and add to the perseveration and knowledge of this exciting craft. I appreciate the input of these authors.

Virtually every known technique in beading can be used, to my amazement by children. They seem to grasp the knowledge very quickly and almost effortlessly begin creating successfully, magnificent, jewelry and ornaments. Their youthful finger dexterity allows them quick and direct movement of the needle and thread. I encourage the youth leaders, of any organization to incorporate beading as part of their craft training. The children will love it and you will make lots of points with the young people.

Vision of a Great Chief

For Applique or embroidery with beads

The beaded Acoma seed pot in this enlargement is shown in the color pages done by Judy Otero of Albuquerque, N.M. The pattern has different geometrics as it goes around the pot. The detail is of original design.

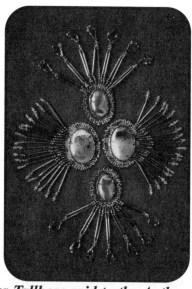

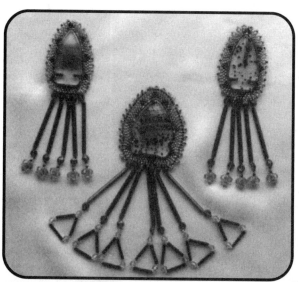

Jennifer Tallbear said to the Author "I have never worked with Montana agate before, but I'll try". Needless to say her creativity excels in each piece she has designed and the photo above reflects her personality.

These beaded Montana Agate arrowheads can be used in any combination of color for a wardrobe. Also by Jennifer. The topaz and emerald green crystals flatter the cabochon .

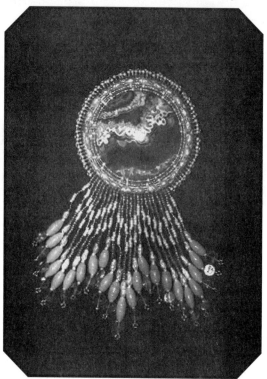

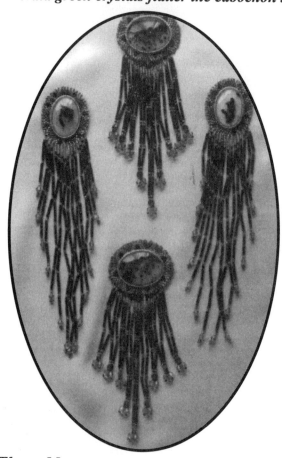

Jennifer graces this crazy lace agate with soft subtle grey's and creamy tan with a splash of white to highlight. The uneven cheverons, of fringes compliments the busy stone and adds a flair of Victorian.

These Montana agate were designed by Jennifer to be placed on a cradle board with other beadwork applique around them.

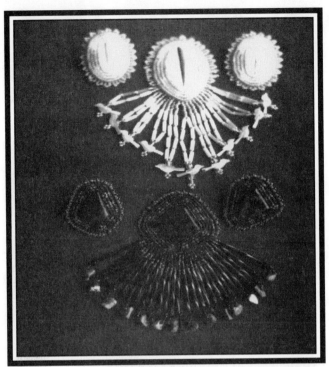

The ghostly looking cabochon in the top of this photograph is called "Fiber Octave" (a man made stone), and the lower set is Azurite-Malachite. All are combined in a lovely combination with beads. by Jennifer Tallbear.

Contrary to the gracefulness of the beautiful stones beaded by Jennifer in this issue the cabochon above displays her ability to go native. American that is! Nicely done, in black, red and silver that compliments the face and head dress.

Margo Fields has put a new twist to her beaded earings. On the right she brings the fringe across an off loomed, slanted body of the earring for an unusual effect. Notice the twisted fringe on the left pair. She has beaded around a fringe row giving it a spiral appearance Great technique Margo.

This lovely beaded pouch was discovered at Custer Battlefield Trading Post, Crow Agency, Mt. The colors are brilliant blue, pink, orange, yellow, green and black.

Beading With Stones

First of all, I would like to welcome you to a lovely, fascinating phase of creating beadwork using stones with glass seed beads. These interesting techniques have a way of completely engulfing you with ideas and style like no other method done before.

When most people think of stones they don't associate the semi-precious stones with good quality jewelry. However, in this chapter, we teach how to incorporate the stone beads and cabochon with glass seed beads to create quality jewelry. You will be able to take advantage of a very exclusive market available for well constructed and original designs.

One of the great advantages in using stones is, you can use the traditional techniques and come up with a Contemporary flair, Classic Victorian or Native American style of beadwork without a lot of readjustment in your original methods.

Creating a pattern for a stone cabochon can be done as you do the beadwork or on graph paper before you begin. In volume five, page 62, we give a brief illustration on using the brickstitch shortcut to your advantage when making a beaded strip to surround a cabochon. That little illustration will save you many hours of beading time if your are making beadwork for sale. We will get into a more extensive teaching of this technique as we cover each aspect of stone beading.

Let's begin by creating an earring using a cabochon. If you don't have two stone cabochon, a pair of pretty flat buttons will do. You will also need a little leather or fabric for backing, some beading thread and needles, fabric or leather glue and, of course, the beads.

For those of you that attend estate sales or garage sales, keep an eye out for ladies kid leather gloves and antique buttons or jewelry made with beads (no plastic). The glove leather is wonderful for backing of a cabochon and the antique buttons can be made into very pretty earrings that are an original. Any necklace made of glass or stone beads can be taken apart and used somewhere in another beading project.

When you have all your materials together, place the cabochon on the leather. Using a large needle or blunt tool, trace around the cabochon. You only want to make an impression of the outline to use as a guide for the glue area. Do not use ink for tracing the cabochon unless the ink is the same color as the beads and cabochon you intend to use. Wet glue may make the ink run on to the cabochon.

Now you can refer to the illustrated instructions "Cabochon Beading Short Cuts" for visual help as we describe the steps in sequence. Using these short cuts can save you a great deal of beading time.

Step #1--Glue the cabochon to the leather using a bead tip cement glue. I prefer L & R Watch Crystal Cement. Place a little glue inside circles traced around the cabochon. Then smooth the glue evenly onto the flat back side of the cabochon. Place the cabochon in the circle and press lightly into place. Take care not to force the glue from between the leather and cabochon. Allow the glue to dry completely before starting your beadwork.

After the glue is dry, carefully trim the leather to within one tenth inch of the cabochon. If you are using a white leather with a dark bead, dye the leather edge. Use a felt tip pen, the color of the bead and carefully color the leather edge. If you dye the leather under the cabochon, you may distort the color of the stone.

Now you can go to step #2. Knot your thread and leave the knot on the backside of the leather. Pick up beads numbered one through four.(ill. plate #2)

Step #3. Pass the needle back through the number one bead (reverse direction) and down through the top side of the leather. Snug the four beads into the position illustrated. Leave the needle and thread on the back side of the leather to begin the next step.

Step #4. Pick up number five bead and pass the needle back through number four bead, (note direction of needle). Now, you have established a foundation and can gain some speed as you complete the next moves.

Step #5. Pick up number six and number seven beads. Pass the needle back though number five bead and through the leather. (illustrated as plate #3) To complete the circle, repeat steps four and five. Pick up one bead and pass the needle back though number seven bead. Pick up two beads and repeat the moves in step five, etc.

Continue around the cabochon.

You are actually beading three rows away from the cabochon at a time. You will want to keep in mind as you bead your pattern that when you first begin this technique, the number three bead becomes the edge bead in step #2. When you get to step #5, the sixth bead becomes the edge bead.

Step #6. Now that you have completed the flat beadwork around the cabochon, create a bezel or slopping edge row of beads around the cabochon. String and attach the row of bezel beads on top of the flat beadwork around the cabochon. Plate #5 illustration shows how the top view of the cabochon should look. Plate #6 shows how the bezel beads rest on the flat beadwork.

Attaching the single line row of bezel beads can be done two ways. First choice-- **string all the line row of bezel beads onto the thread and measure the strung beads around the cabochon.** Pass the needle back through the first four beads, connecting the circle. Attach every other bead of the circle to the leather by going down through the leather and coming up in place, as illustrated in plate #7. Take care not to pull the stitches so tight that it separates the flat beadwork from the cabochon. The bezel must rest on top of the flat beadwork, yet still be secure.

Second choice-- **attach the line row of bezel beads, three beads at a time, as illustrated in plate #7.** After you have all the beads in place, pass the needle back through all the beads in the bezel row and snug them close together. This will place them firmly around and slightly higher on the cabochon. Secure by knotting through the leather. Place a dab of clear nail polish on the knot.

In order to add another row of brickstitch to the flat beadwork, you must omit the edge bead illustrated in steps two through five. Plate #8 shows how the first two rows go on together. Then you can add the third row of brickstitch to your pattern, including the edge bead at the same time, as

The Finished earring is shown on the front of this volume. The Dendrite Agate earring in progress has a different moss pattern in the cabochon because it it virtually impossible to find two dendrite agate formations exactly the same. However when the beadwork is complete they will be a recognizable pair. Notice the dyed black leather edge the beads are being attached to as they are picked up and placed around the cabochon. On the finished earring there is a constant row of burgundy beads around the bottom, vee half, of the cabochon. (After all other beadwork was completed,) These beads were attached last by passing the needle through a burgundy edge bead and picking up another edge bead before passing the needle through the next edge bead. This fills in the spaces between the edge beads making a solid row of beads. The solid row of beads also holds the fringes down and inline with the outside brickstitch row on which the fringes are connected.

illustrated in plate #9. Fringe is optional. However, stone beads on fringe adds a lot of personality and enchanting radiance to the finished piece.

There are lots of options available on how to use beadwork with cabochon. In this chapter we will cover methods used by this author.

If you prefer to do the beadwork first then attach it around the cabochon, there are short cuts for that method also. For a visual glimpse of the steps described in the following paragraphs turn to the illustrated page entitled "The Simplicity Of Brickstitch Used with Cabochon".

Plates #12 and #13 show a simple three row strip of beadwork which can be attached to the same amount of leather edge used in plate #1. This strip of beadwork is connected to the leather by using the whip stitch through the row of beads nearest the cabochon.

When designing an unusual shape around a cabochon such as a flower or fan, you will need enough background material (leather) around the cabochon to applique the complete piece of beadwork in place.

A half circle of beadwork for a fan can be made before you attach the beadwork around the cabochon. Using the two row step illustrated in plate #13, makes quick work out of a time consuming project.

Creating a fan shape; Step #1-- Decide what size fan you want your finished piece to be and make a paper pattern. You will need enough leather to make two patterns, one for the front and one to cover the back. Lay the pattern on the leather and trace around the pattern with a tracing wheel. **Do not cut them out yet.** Lay the cabochon in place, inside the fan pattern and trace around it. Next glue the cabochon into place and set aside to dry.

Step #2--Using the two row step illustrated in plates # 13 & 13-A, make a beaded strip of two rows long enough to reach two thirds way around the cabochon.

Step #3-- For the next row allow a little slack in the thread for looser stitches and add a single row of brickstitch to the strip omitting the edge bead as illustrated below in plate # 14. The slack in this row will allow the beadwork to form a fan around the cabochon without to much stress, which would pull it into a bowl like position if the beads are to tight.

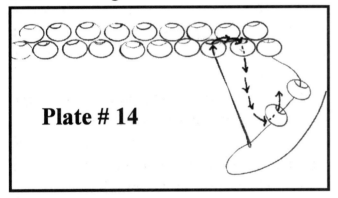

Plate # 14

To begin the single row pick up two beads and pass the needle through the third bead of the existing row and back up through the second bead. Now you are in line to complete a single row of brickstitch the length of your strip, one bead at a time.

Step #4--For the next row add the edge bead along with the the row of brickstitch as illustrated in plate #9.

In order to get the fan look that Jennifer Tallbear achieved with the round pink rhodochrosite stone, shown in the color section of this volume, you must do a little applique next to the cabochon and put a bezel line of beads around the cabochon. As you can see from the black and white photo below, the round cabochon was glued

to the fan pattern of leather, then the fresh water pearls were attached in place with needle and thread through the leather, before appliqued around with size 14/0 beads.

Next arrange the beaded strip in a rainbow arch above the appliqued stone and attach the strip to the leather and the appliqued beadwork by sewing down through the leather and up, passing the needle through one of the appliqued beads and one of the strip beads before going down through the leather again. The leather fan pattern should be large enough to place the beaded strip on and serve as a backing for appliqueing the strip into place.

Step # 5-- You have already added an edge bead to the strip. Do not sew the edge bead to the leather pattern. Instead, being careful not to cut any threads, cut the leather fan pattern out now, allowing the edge bead to extend out past the pattern edge. Cut the leather back pattern out also. These two pattern pieces have to be exactly the same size.

Step # 6-- Glue the pin back in place to the back of the beaded fan. Take note that the pin back is glued right side up. After the glue drys, place the back leather pattern the glue drys, place the back leather pattern in place on the back side of the beaded fan and press an impression of the pin back into the leather. Make a small hole in the leather where the impression indicates the pin bail should come through and one for the pin to come through. The base shank of the pin back will be covered with leather.

Step # 7--Brush leather glue evenly over the back side of the beaded fan. Make sure you are placing the glue on the proper side of the back pattern piece and spread the glue evenly onto the back pattern of leather. Allow the glue to dry to a tackier consistency, then stick the bail and pin, in place through the holes in the leather and press the leather into place, covering the complete back of the fan.

After the glue is dry, carefully trim the edges of the leather patterns to the same size.

Step #7-- Now you are ready to add the final edge stitch or extend the beadwork a little further out on the fan by adding more rows of brickstitch . Which ever you decide to do you will need to connect through both pieces of leather.

For the final edge stitch use steps #2 and #3, illustrated in plate #2, going completely around the fan including the cabochon. Allow the edge bead from the beaded strip to over lap the final edge stitch to give a ruffle look to the fan.

If you have decided to extend your beadwork, use the step illustrated plate # 8 then go to plate # 9 for adding another row with the final edge stitch.

You can use the two bead strips in so many different ways. It can be connected

directly to the leather around the cabochon and single rows can be attached as illustrated in plate # 15 below. When adding this

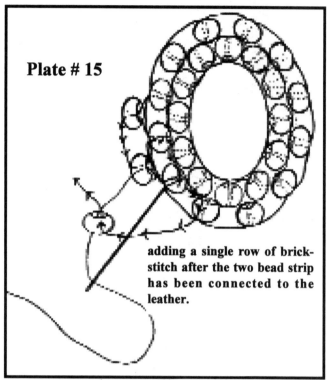

Plate # 15

adding a single row of brick-stitch after the two bead strip has been connected to the leather.

row, remember to allow a little slack in your stitches.

If you want a leather backing behind the beadwork, don't trim the leather until you are ready to edge stitch. Then connect the leather and beadwork together with the final edge beaded row. Don't forget to add the bezel row to cover the edge of the cabochon.

If you are afraid the cabochon may come loose from the beadwork, then after the project is completely finished, carefully apply a **very small** amount of super glue between the bezel row and cabochon. Do not let the super glue run down through the beads or get on the cabochon or all your work may be in vain. Allow the super glue to dry completely before moving the beadwork to avoid getting the glue in the wrong area.

The earrings above were done by Doris Barnes

Notice how Doris Barnes has used another short cut in arranging the beads around her cabochon earrings.

She begins her earrings by gluing the ear post directly to the back side of the cabochon. Next she cuts the leather for the back of the cabochon and makes a small hole for the ear post to stick through and glues the leather to the back of the cabochon.

Before she begins to bead, she allows the glue to dry and trims the leather to within two bead rows away from the cabochon and dyes the leather edge the same color as her beads and thread.

For the beadwork, Doris circles the cabochon with beads, attaching every third bead as illustrated in plate # 7. Next she anchors an edge stitch through the leather and through the outside bead row, completely around the cabochon.

For a different look on two of the earrings, Doris has created a flower using an off loom technique and attached it across the cabochon to the beaded circle. On another she has attached the stems of two beaded flowers to the beadwork arranged around the cabochon and glued the flowers directly onto the cabochon. Needless to say that the fringe enhances the stones and adds complimenting colors to the earrings.

Notice in the photo, the bottom middle stone center, is an unusual shape, however Doris has managed to form three rows of beads around the stone (a crystal concho from Brazil) using the method described above. Then glued fresh water pearls to the inside crystals of the stone creating a lovely oyster shell effect to the earring.

Doris continues to come up with new ideas in her beading techniques and has established a good market for her crafts.

To create an elegant necklace, use any one of the cabochon techniques illustrated for the center piece and connect a neckline using a single strand of stone beads to each side of the beaded cabochon. Stone beads hang better if you knot between each bead or use a small bead in place of the knot. It is best to use the silk or nylon beading thread especially designed for stringing larger beads rather then tiger tail wire with crimp beads . The tiger tail is not as free moving as beading cord and has a tendency to kink and break sometimes. The stone beads need room to move in order to avoid becoming chipped and scratched against each other.

To add a clasp to the back of the necklace, use a finding called a" knot cover bead". Place the knot cover bead over the knot and crimp closed with needle nose pliers. The clasp can be connected directly to the knot cover bead or you can add another finding called a "jump ring" in between.

I prefer to make the neckline long enough to go over my head and not have to put a clasp on. However that makes the neckline at least eighteen inches circumference and a large center piece looks better on a shorter length neckline.

Throughout the years I have tried a lot of different things in beadwork that I thought would cut the beading time down. Some of them worked and many of them cost me more time in unscrambling the mess then doing it the original way.

One of the good, little secrets that I have discovered in my trials is the use of Scotch double coated tape by 3M. This tape is great for holding beadwork into place while you applique it on to leather or fabric. It frees your hands to use the needle and thread and helps prevent that ever, unforgiving, winkle in the beaded strip that shows up when the project is finished.

I leave it under the beadwork permanently. You don't have to worry about messy glue coming up through the beads. It holds long pieces of beaded strips in place on belts, sleeves, legging sides, yokes, and any other positions, while you sew them on. One of the greatest uses is holding a hatband on a hat. That is the one strip of beadwork I never sew on anymore. I attach it right to the hat with the tape and just change the tape when it gets old enough to let go.

I'm not suggesting you use the tape to hold beadwork on, without sewing it on. You may loose the beadwork, but you can save a lot of time by using this tape as an extra hand, even on the smallest projects. There are certain things it should not be used for. It will not hold a cabochon on, or hold a leather hem up on a garment permanently, But I'm sure you will find dozens of other uses for it in your crafts.

There are so many devises on the market that make claims of doing fantastic things to help you in your crafts, you get a little gun shy after investing in a few that don't do what they claim.

There is a particular bead sizing device that I can honestly say works great and does everything that it promises to do. It is called a Size-O-Matic and it really does work, even with the small size seed beads. Allen Graves developed the Size-O-Matic. I quote him in saying "It is important to cull your beads! Discard any that are irregular as they will detract from the over all appearance of your finished piece". I agree and Allen Graves, Size-O-Matic, will sort, cull and size seed beads, to your amazement. Unicorn Beading Supply Co. 4326 SE Woodstock-Box 390, Portland, Or. 97206-6270, will get you more information about this great devise.

Allen also offers a great set of templates for bead patterns. He is working to perfect a rosette template and will make it available to the public very soon. The rosette patterns designed in this volume are done by the author on Allen's newly developing rosette graph.

The beautiful dendrite agate cabochon

The beautiful dendrite agate cabochon shown on the front cover and below are very rare. At one time they were afforded only to the royalty of India. Each dendrite forms a fern like formation resembling trees and unusual fiery scenes at sunset. Each one is completely different from any other. As you can see from the six cabochon shown below, each one has a different scene in it and each holds its place in beauty. It is very difficult to choose which to bead around and what colors to use for fear of taking away some of the elegance from the stone. However, the Author wanted to share with you that any stone can be used with beads. A lot of people limit their choice of color in stones available because they believe a solid color stone is best for beading. There are beautiful stones that are many colors within the same cabochon but that does not make them less valuable. Quite the contrary. The Montana Moss agate is a very busy colored stone, similar the dendrite cabochon below, yet are affordable and available through most rock shops. The state of Texas also has a beautiful plume agate. Many are found in Oregon and other parts of the U.S.A. You may be surprised at the stones you walk over everyday.

Rare dendrite cabochon used on front cover beadwork

Cabochon Beading Short Cuts

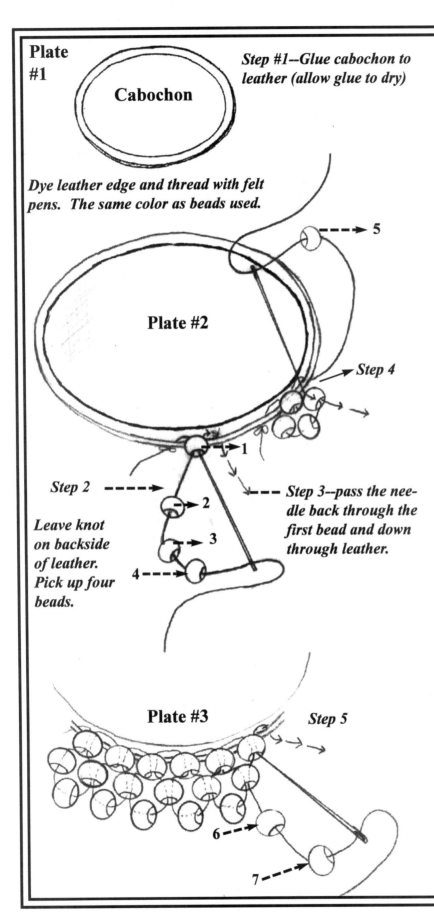

Plate #1

Cabochon

Step #1--Glue cabochon to leather (allow glue to dry)

Dye leather edge and thread with felt pens. The same color as beads used.

Plate #2

→ 5

→ Step 4

→ 1

Step 2 ---→

2

3

4 ---→

Leave knot on backside of leather. Pick up four beads.

Step 3--pass the needle back through the first bead and down through leather.

Plate #3

Step 5

6 ---→

7 ---→

The illustrated steps on these two pages can save hours of beading time. When done as directed, you are actually beading three rows at a time. Bead #3 becomes the edge bead in step #2.

When you get to step #5, bead #6 becomes the edge bead for the rest of the circumference of the cabochon.

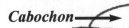

Cabochon ———→

Side view of domed cabochon glue to leather.

Plate #4

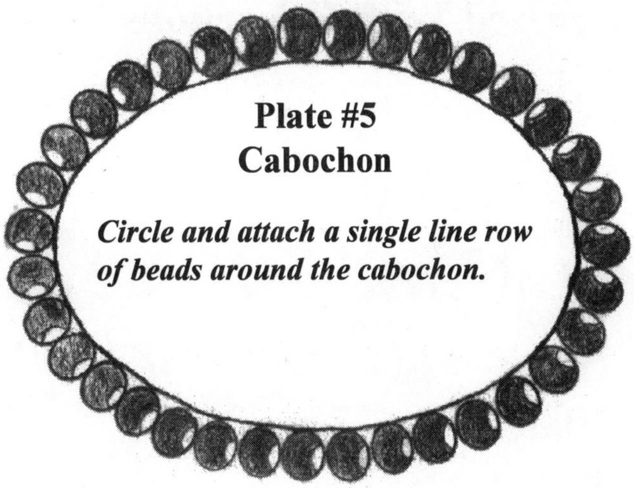

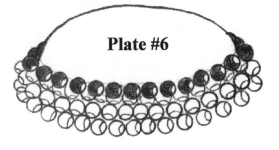

Plate #5
Cabochon

Circle and attach a single line row of beads around the cabochon.

Single line row of beads rests on top of finished edge beads and covers cabochon edge.

Plate #6

Plate #7

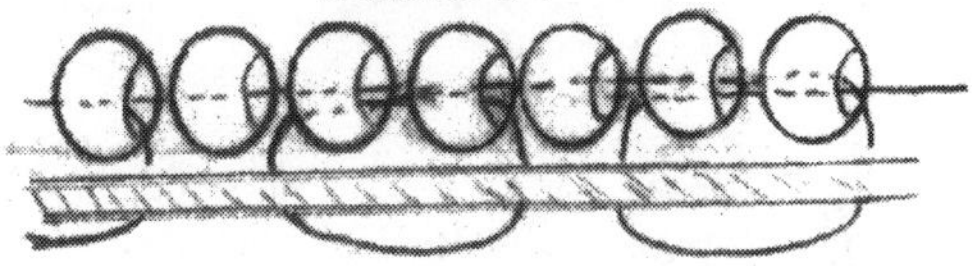

(Attaching Single Line Row)

Attach single line row of beads around cabochon. Take care not to snug the line so tight that it separates the finished edge beads from the cabochon. When you have finished attaching the single line row of beads, pass your needle and thread back through the complete circle of beads and snug them closely together. This will place them firmly around and slightly higher on the cabochon. Secure by knotting through the leather. Place a dab of clear nail polish on the knot.

Plate #8

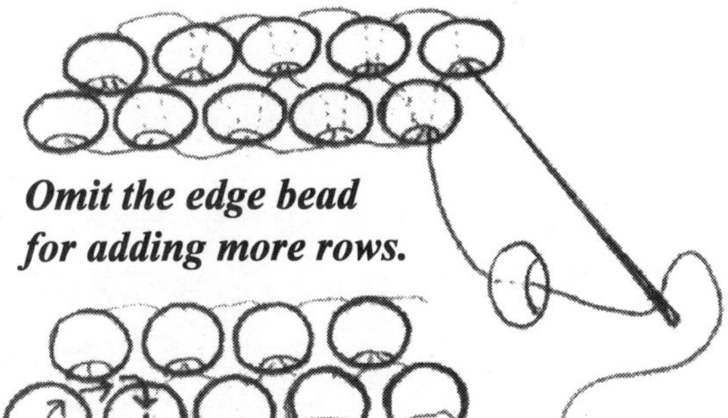

Omit the edge bead for adding more rows.

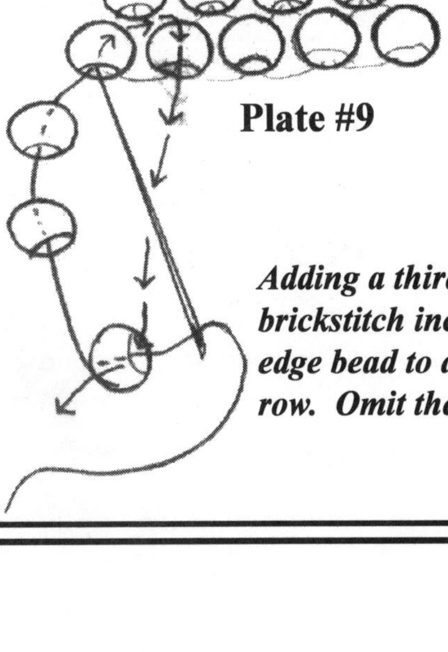

Plate #9

Adding a third row of brickstitch including edge bead to add a 5th row. Omit the edge bead.

The Simplicity Of Brickstitch
Used With Cabochons

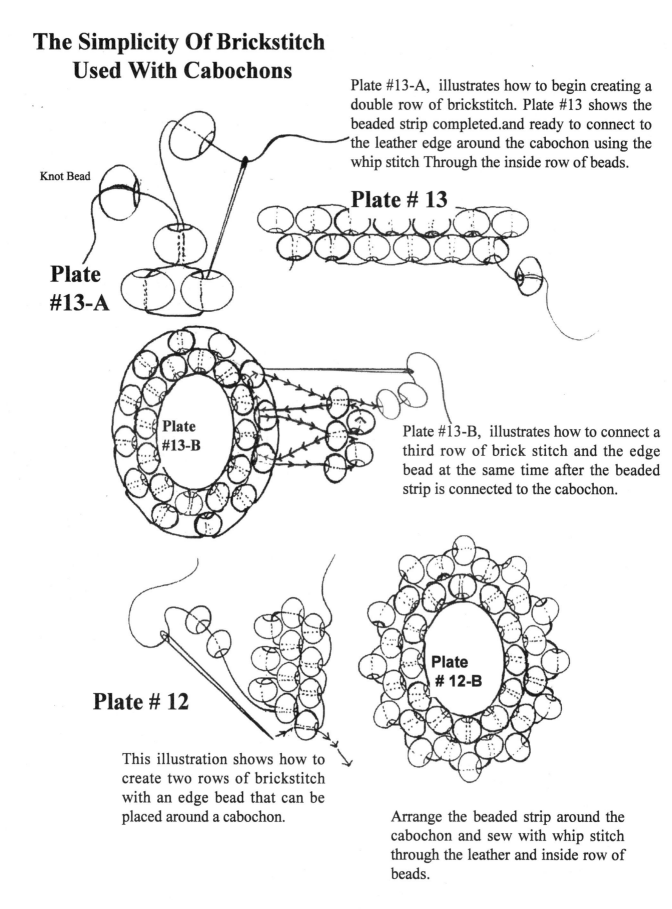

Plate #13-A, illustrates how to begin creating a double row of brickstitch. Plate #13 shows the beaded strip completed.and ready to connect to the leather edge around the cabochon using the whip stitch Through the inside row of beads.

Plate # 13

Knot Bead

Plate #13-A

Plate #13-B

Plate #13-B, illustrates how to connect a third row of brick stitch and the edge bead at the same time after the beaded strip is connected to the cabochon.

Plate # 12

Plate # 12-B

This illustration shows how to create two rows of brickstitch with an edge bead that can be placed around a cabochon.

Arrange the beaded strip around the cabochon and sew with whip stitch through the leather and inside row of beads.

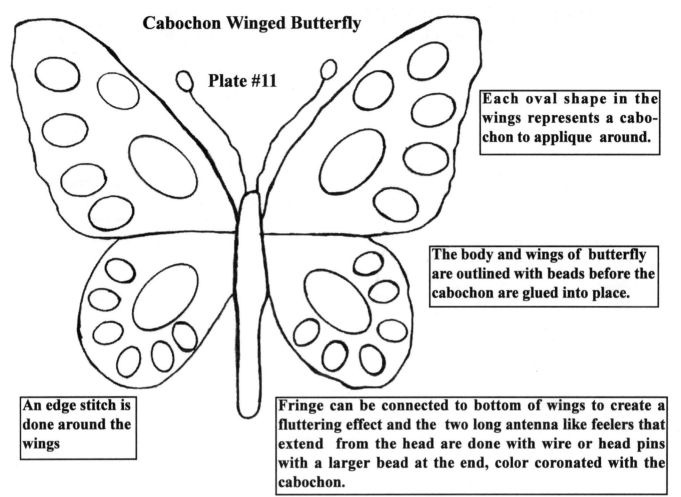

Cabochon Winged Butterfly

Plate #11

Each oval shape in the wings represents a cabochon to applique around.

The body and wings of butterfly are outlined with beads before the cabochon are glued into place.

An edge stitch is done around the wings

Fringe can be connected to bottom of wings to create a fluttering effect and the two long antenna like feelers that extend from the head are done with wire or head pins with a larger bead at the end, color coronated with the cabochon.

The elusive butterfly has been done in beadwork hundreds of ways, but one of the most beautiful is created with stone cabochon, appliqued into place with glass seed beads. The pattern above illustrates how to get started using the techniques already discussed previously in this chapter. To begin the butterfly, you will need beading leather or a fabric that will support the weight of the cabochon without folding. To many folds or bends will cause the cabochon to pop out before they are secured with beaded and glued bezel rows.

When you are working with a lot of cabochon in the same project, I have found it quicker and less troublesome to do most of the beadwork before gluing the cabochon into place.

Step #1-- Trace or draw the outline of the butterfly and cabochon placements on the leather. Trace a back pattern outline also.

Step #2--Outline and applique with glass seed beads, as much of the pattern as possible, including the body, before gluing on the cabochon. Allow the glue to dry completely before going the next step.

Step #3--Bead a bezel row around each cabochon and complete the rest of the applique work. Connect the wire feelers.

Step #4--Glue the back pattern into place. Carefully trim the leather pattern edges evenly. Do an edge stitch around the butterfly and add fringe to the bottom of the wings with a stone turn bead.

Cowboy Hat Cabochon Earring

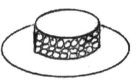

Side view of cowboy hat with beaded hat band.

Plate #16

Plate#17

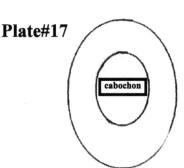

Top View of cowboy hat with a 20x15 size cabochon.

Plate #18

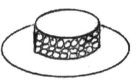

Step # 1

Cut a leather strip 2 1/3 inches long by 1/3 in. wide for circle.

make hole for ear post

Step #4--Cut an oval of leather the desired size of the hat brim and do an edge stitch around it. Make a pin hole in top center of the inside circle for ear post.

Leather circle should be same size as cabochon.

Plate #19

Plate # 21

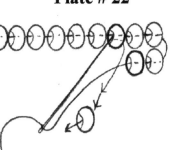

Step # 2--Lap and glue the end of the leather strip 1/3 inch and allow to dry completely

Step #3- Cut three leather disks the same size as the cabochon (20x15) and glue them together firmly.

Plate #20

Plate # 22

Follow written instructions on the opposite page for assembling of the cowboy hat earring.

Step # 5--Make an off loom beaded strip four beads wide by two inches long To be placed around the dome of the hat for a hat band.

The cowboy hat earring is unique because of the size and exact likeness of the real hat. It's made of leather and has a beaded hatband, however the top of the crown is where the cabochon rests. To begin this project you will need beading leather, crystal cement and leather glue, a cabochon (size 20x15) or a button that measures 2 in. around. A small size seed bead is used for more detail in the hat band. Size 13/0 cut beads adds sparkle. Beading and glover needles and thread. Kevlar thread should not be used near the chemicals in glue or any other chemicals. It is a great, almost unbreakable thread for beading projects that will not be exposed to chemicals and I use it for lots of beadwork, especially fringe. For this project use the nymo beading thread.

Step # 1--Cut a leather strip 2 1/3 inches long by 1/3 inch wide. This strip will support the cabochon and beaded strip.

Step #2--Lap the leather strip 1/3 inch and glue into a circle, as illustrated. Make sure the circle is the exact size of your cabochon.

Step #3-- Cut three leather disks the same size as the cabochon. Trace around the cabochon for size and cut traced line off for an accurate measure. Glue the three disks firmly together in a layered stack. Allow the glue to dry completely.

Step #4--Cut an oval of leather the desired size of the hat brim and do an edge stitch around it. Trace around the cabochon in the middle of the oval, as illustrated. Make a pin hole for the earring post to go through. Place a little glue around the pin hole and insert the ear post. To hang the earring from a ear wire, omit the pin hole and make a five bead circle, connected to the edge stitch for the ear wire.

Step #5--Make an off loom beaded strip two inches long by four beads wide. If you are using a larger bead then suggested, you may not need four rows wide. Measure the beads according to the width of the leather strip. This strip will represent the hatband. Add beaded fringe last.

Step #6--This step is not illustrated. Using a glover needle (leather needle), sew the leather circle (the dome of the hat) into place on the brim. Use a close whip stitch to sew the leather circle to the traced pattern of the cabochon in the center of the leather oval. The leather circle should surround the back plate of the ear post.

Step #7--Using the crystal cement glue. Glue the leather disks down into the leather circle. Spread the cement glue evenly but not to liberally, over the back metal disk of the ear post and inside the circle. Press the disks into place. Be careful not to force the glue out of the circle. The cabochon is going to rest on these disks, so be sure they are glued in well and allow the glue to dry completely.

Step # 8-- Glue the cabochon into place on top of the leather disks. The cabochon should rest slightly down in the leather circle. Next, arrange the beaded strip (hatband) around the leather circle and sew into place through the brim of the hat.

Step #9--Make a bezel row of beads around the cabochon. Sew to the top of the leather circle. Spot glue a small amount of cement around the bezel row to secure.

Stone Bead Sleeve Earring

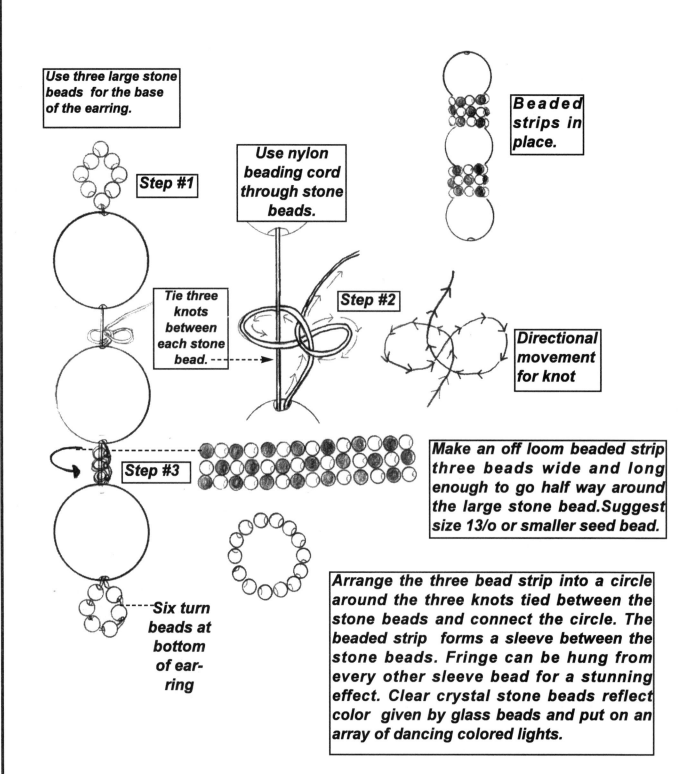

Use three large stone beads for the base of the earring.

Step #1

Use nylon beading cord through stone beads.

Tie three knots between each stone bead.

Step #2

Beaded strips in place.

Directional movement for knot

Step #3

Make an off loom beaded strip three beads wide and long enough to go half way around the large stone bead. Suggest size 13/o or smaller seed bead.

Six turn beads at bottom of ear- ring

Arrange the three bead strip into a circle around the three knots tied between the stone beads and connect the circle. The beaded strip forms a sleeve between the stone beads. Fringe can be hung from every other sleeve bead for a stunning effect. Clear crystal stone beads reflect color given by glass beads and put on an array of dancing colored lights.

Maiden Earring Pattern

Braids are 13 blk. long,with W,X,W color for hair tie and 5 blk. for turn beads.

Step #6

The head of the maiden is done with the loom-beading without-a-loom technique also known as the square stitch. This technique is illustrated in volumes #3 and #4.

Step #1

Step #2

Edge stitch in red around the head for crown

Color chart
X..........Aqua blue
W.........Red
O..........White
/............Flesh
Hair and braids are black. (blk.)
Mouth...Red

Step#3

Upper body is brickstitched then connected to the neck. The blue beads on neck represent earrings.

Middle of body is square stitch of 4 beads wide by 11 beads long. The arms are connected last to the top of the waist line. The 6 flesh beads at the end of the left arm form a circle to represent the hands. The right arm crosses the front and connects the the hand circle.

Step #4

Step #7

Step #5

The bottom of the body is brickstitched, 11 across 8 deep, then connected to the waist band. For the skirt add a fringe on each side of the eight rows of brickstitch and across the bottom 18 fringes total. Use 21 beads and one turn bead for the skirt fringe. The skirt fringe will flare like a fan and form the skirt.

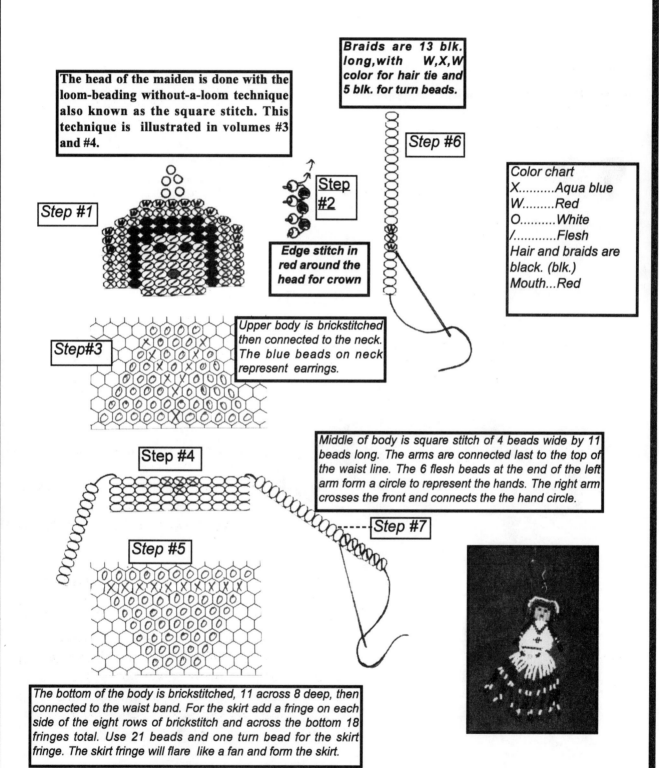

Boy and Girl makes a Pair of Corn Dance, Sand Painting, Earring Pattern

The earrings can be made using an off loom square stitch, reducing and increasing where needed for detail. (see volume #3 for off loom instructions);Loom-beading-without-a-loom).

Two fringes of yellow and green beads connects to the wrist of each hand on the boy and girl.

Girls braid connects to her hair at the shoulder line and hangs on the front of the pattern.

Boys top is constructed just like the girl. The boys waist connects on same line illustrated for second earring.

Toni Acedo has incorporated these blue glass cabochons with muted browns, blues, and yellows in a star burst effect. Lovely.

In Volume Eight, we exposed the chili earrings by Toni Acedo of Toni's Earrie Delights. And in this volume we show the red chili necklace. Quite a "hot" design!!

Suzanne Myre of Ellis, Kansas has beaded the infamous "End of Trails" design. SuOriginals is just getting off the ground--but what a great start!

Tamera Dickerson has beaded these peyote stitch earrings in a variety of colors all with accents of black, gold, and white. On the top left, blue is the primary color. Top right--purple. Bottom left--red. Bottom right--turquoise.

Ella Johnson-Bentley of Juneau, Alaska has created some unique designs in her latest beading projects. A local potter is making Tlingit Totemic mask buttons and Ella has incorporated these into her bead-work. The cabochon pins are done in greens, pinks and blues--beautiful! The necklace purse on ultra suede (on right) has been beaded with a potpourri of flowers.

"LOOMING HELP" for large projects created on small looms

So many times people write in to ask, "How do you go about creating a large loom project on a small loom, without having the finished project look like a patchwork quilt? After connecting small pieces of loom work together the threads always look like an after thought."

There are some simple steps that make this problem much easier. In order to understand this technique better, I suggest you begin with a pattern only twice as wide as your loom will hold.

First, in planning your project determine how many beads across your loom will hold and how many beads across your pattern. If your loom will hold half the pattern across then you are in good shape.

Step #1- **Omit the center vertical row** of your pattern and string your loom for half the pattern. If your loom is long enough to loom both halves without restringing then you have saved some time. Examine the sample pattern below. The arrow is center vertical row of pattern.

The secret to this technique is omitting the connecting row. The next illustration shows how to bead both halves of the pattern with the double warp on one side of the loom. The second half (bottom) of the pattern is loomed upside down.

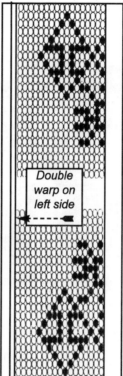

Double warp on left side

After you have completed both halves of the pattern, omitting the center, vertical row. Tape across the warp threads, between and on each end of the patterns. Remove the beadwork from the loom and cut the two finished pieces apart. Connect them with the missing row of beads, one bead at a time. The double warp thread ends up on both sides of the beadwork when you turn the bottom side of the pattern up right.

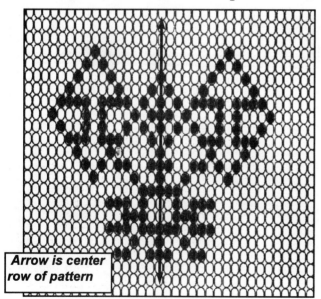

Arrow is center row of pattern

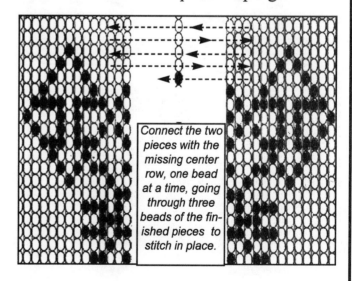

Connect the two pieces with the missing center row, one bead at a time, going through three beads of the finished pieces to stitch in place.

Sheri Nelson Creations

Sheri Nelson is a very talented beader from Central, Alaska. She calls her beading and craft business "Cabin Fever Gifts" As you can see, she takes advantage of the long winters in Alaska.

The upper right; photo is a Yakima maiden beaded on a leather pouch purse. **The upper left;**A beautiful rose appliqued onto a red hand bag. **The lower left**; A native totem design of Alaska "humming bird and whale". **The lower right;** "whale and raven totem".

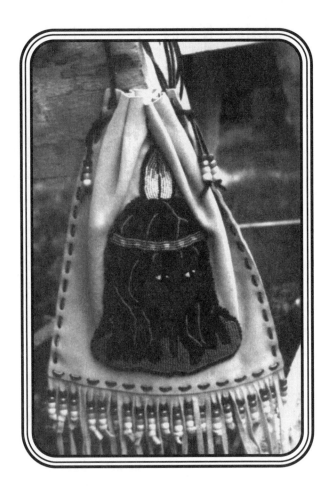

SHERI NELSON'S hands are apparently never idle, nor does she lack for imaginative ideas for her patterns in beading. The two husky dogs above, the rattle snake moccasins and the grizzly bear below, indicate Sheri is a real animal lover and I admire her choice of residence. Alaska stands out in her beading.

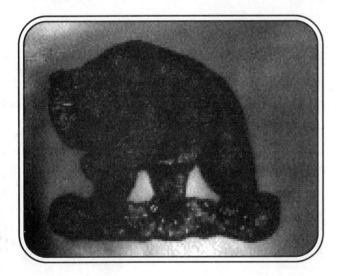

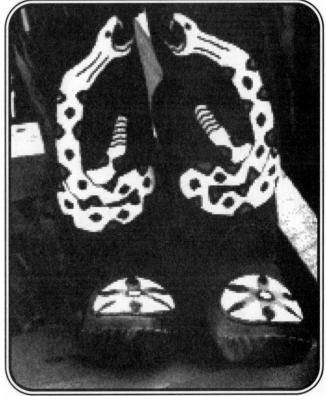

Southwestern for Applique

 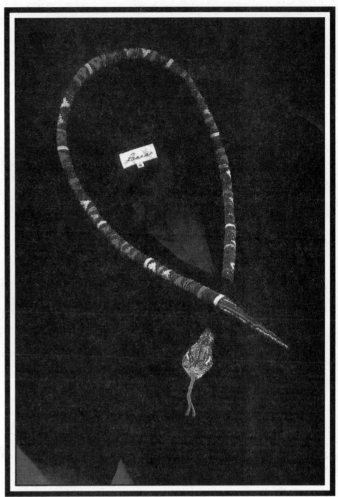

Susan Cochran is a very accomplished beader. I am one of her great admirers. Her ideas are always new and refreshing, giving extensive detail to large beaded pieces on appliqued garments. The photos above attest to her versatility. The little buckskin teddy bear would be a welcomed addition to any doll collector. She has traditional details that include a hand made knife, peace pipe, bow and arrows with quiver and she has even added a concho belt with the beadwork. Lucky child that received this gift.

Susan has been gracious enough to share her work with us throughout this series and has inspired many beaders to attempt her style of beading. Her patterns range from Native American through African, contemporary, and European styles. We show a full color page of Susan's beadwork in this issue which will give an idea of the volume of her work. One of the most noble gestures comes from Susan in the form of a charitable heart. She does not sell her work but donates most of it to different organizations to help others. I tip my hat to you Susan Cochran.

Notice the beautiful snake around the collar and lapel of the jacket above. The jacket front is closed, yet the head and tail of the snake is in full view. A lot of thought went into this design. The snake head goes through the closure of the jacket.

My Friend for applique technique

—

A closer look at Melody Abbott's latest breathtaking creation

This portion of the gun scabbard shows an Alaskan Native American pattern with a polar bear at its feet, there is a beaded claw hanging

A background of white tree line shows off a horse with a wolf nipping at his nose.

The middle portion of the pattern has a native face with blowing hair. Below is an eagle claw

My friend Melody Abbott has set her needle and beads to work again on a breathtaking array of patterns, loom beaded and placed on gun scabbards and purses.

The photographs on this page are a close up of one of the scabbards shown in the color pages of this volume. How does she do it so fast and accurate, you ask?

When trying to describe Melody's extensive patterns, words are just not good enough, so I show some of her large pieces in sections to allow you a little closer look at her wonderful talent.

Melody and her family have retired to a lovely wilderness area in Colorado. She beads during winter months or when she isn't gardening, riding horses or preparing for winter. You are an amazing lady Melody. We envy you.

Shalimar Tracy

SHALIMAR TRACY beaded these Peacock earrings from a pattern designed by Sigrid Wynn Evans "Earrings by Sig" They feature translucent opalescent ab crystals. Done in sz. 15/o seed beads.

SHALIMAR uses "Sig's" pattern again in the lovely Amazon parrot set above, with metallic silver beads, spiral bugle, cobalt blue crystals and hand painted beads.

Navajo Yei, sand painting figure, bolo tie loomed by Shalimar. Done in size 15/o beads, backed with leather.

Loomed Rug style bolo tie, created by SHALIMAR, done in three tiered effect. Tips are hand made and sewn onto the cord. (1993 State Fair Entry).

Quills
Feathers
&
Beads

Quilled flower in center of applique

Words cannot describe this beautifully quilled, hand painted imitation eagle feather, done by SIMONE TAPIA. Watch for more of Simone's work in the color pages of volume # 10. Perhaps she will share her technique with us.

SIMONE TAPIA, of "The Little Eagle Trading Post" in West Palm Beach Fl., has done the delicate, quill worked bracelet above with natural color dyed quills, dyed by her in red, blue and white.

Designing A Rosette

One of the easiest ways I have found to create a precisely beaded rosette, resembles a pie pattern. Designing a slice at a time. The illustration on this page will give you a visual idea of what I mean by slice.

Begin by drawing a circle on the background material (preferably beading leather). If you are using fabric or felt, I suggest you place interfacing on the back and front of the fabric to give a better foundation to work on. The interfacing will also keep the threads from pulling through.

Next, color the background with felt tip pens, the same color as your beading pattern and beads. Divide the circle into eight slices. Attach a center bead, then circle it with eight beads, attaching every other bead. Now you have completed the center of your rosette.

Using the slice lines as guides, bead each line. Take note as to the direction of the hole in the bead. Since the beadwork works in a circle, you will want the holes to go in a circle also. Use the whip stitch to attach each line bead one at a time.

After you have beaded each guide line out to the circumference of your pattern, fill each slice in, one at a time. You can extend your pattern by making your guide lines longer, than filling in each slice as you go.

Converting your nine center beads to a cabochon gives your rosette an elegant look. You can also add cabochon in each slice and bead around them, creating a pattern within a pattern.

If you are making a pin or bolo tie, glue the finding in place onto the back of the rosette. Cut a round piece of background material, then cut the proper holes for the shanks of the finding to go through. Place the shanks of the finding through the holes and glue the round piece of background material to the back side. After the glue dries, do an edge stitch around the rosette. The edge stitch covers the edge and will secure the background material to the front.

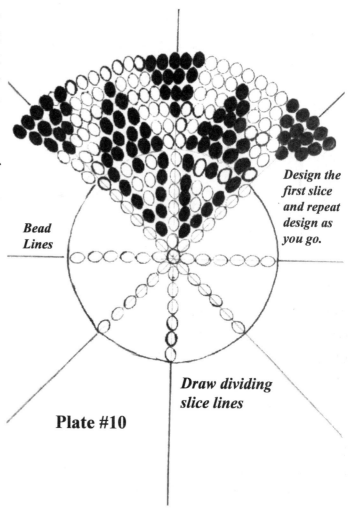

Bead Lines

Design the first slice and repeat design as you go.

Draw dividing slice lines

Plate #10

Fringing is optional, but when a stone bead is added to fringe, you have added an elegant look to your beaded rosette.

I'm very thankful to Allen Graves for allowing me to introduce his new rosette template to you. Bead people have needed this time saving graph for a long time. It can be used for designing around cabochon and it helps take the guess work out of spacing beads . You will have a good idea of what your finished piece will look like.

I found it especially useful for some of the South Western patterns I have wanted to do for ages but didn't have the time to graph them for rosette. Allen will make this template available to the public soon.

Most of the following rosette designs in this chapter are from baskets of the traditional Native American weave used across this continent. My mother has used these designs successfully in her beaded rosettes for hair barrett's and ties.

One of the most helpful hints in designing a rosette is making sure all your beads are the same size before you begin your project. Cull out any odd or distorted shapes that might hinder the size of your pattern.

Since the beads go around rather then across, geometric designs are difficult to fit into the form. It becomes necessary sometimes to add or subtract the number of beads it takes to match the pattern on all sides. As long as you keep your pattern outline in prospective, you can add or subtract the necessary beads from the background color to make the pattern outline, line up with the circle.   Sometimes this makes more background beads on one side than the other, but it will not be as noticeable as long as the outline of the pattern is in place.

On some of the rosette patterns illustrated you will find a slight variation in the equal number of beads in the background from one side to the other. However the subject of the pattern appears to be in line.

So don't be to concerned about the exact amount of beads used in the geometrics of rosette beading. Fill in the proper color on the proper area, according to the measurements or outline of your pattern subject and let the background beads absorb the imbalance number of beads. In the long run you have saved a lot of time and chances are the background count will never be noticed, unless someone is trying to duplicate your work.

43

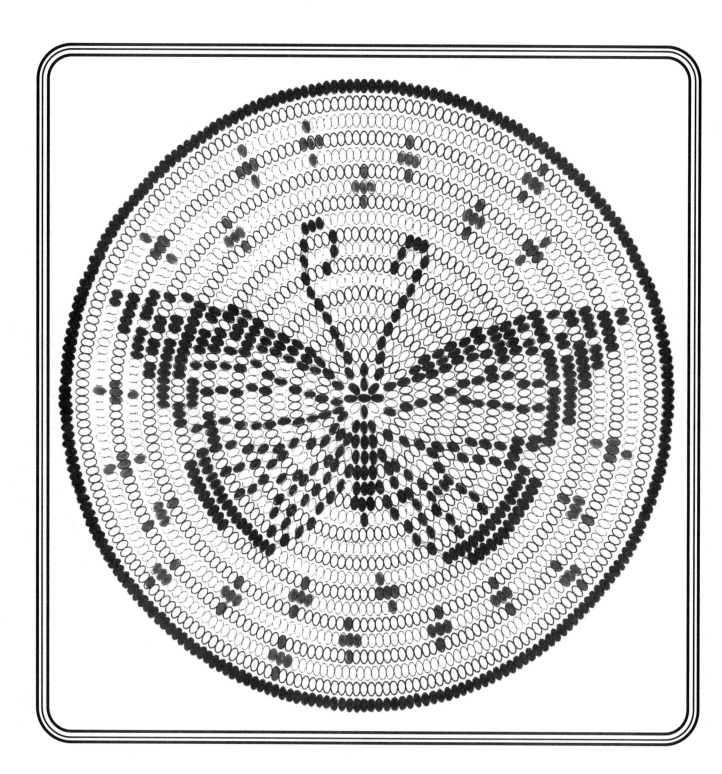

Butterfly Rosette

Hanging fringe gives movement look to butterfly

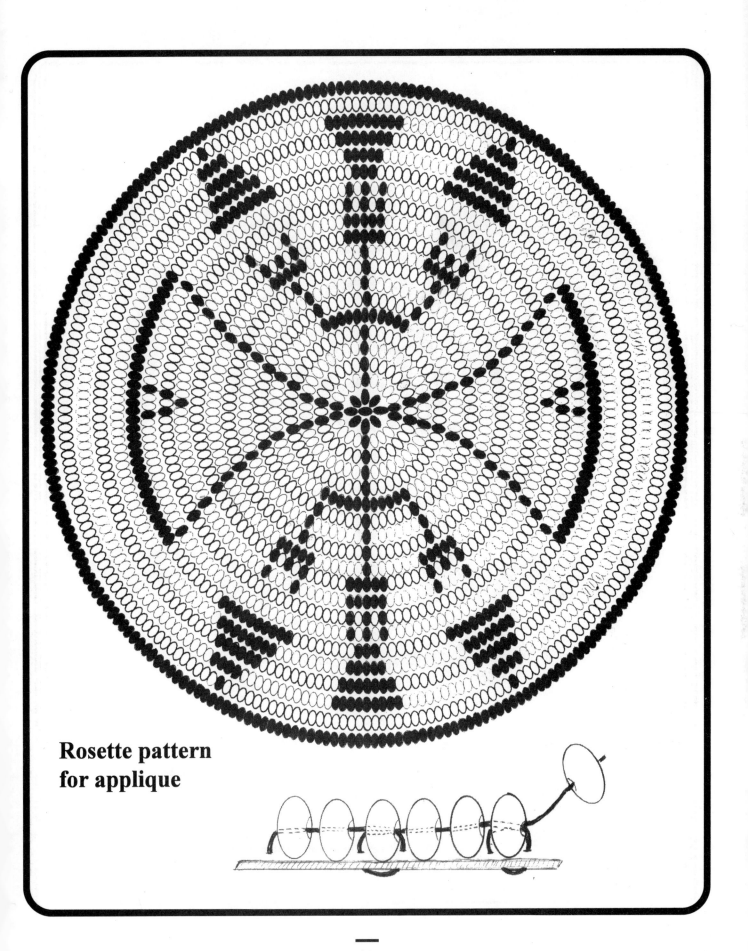

**Rosette pattern
for applique**

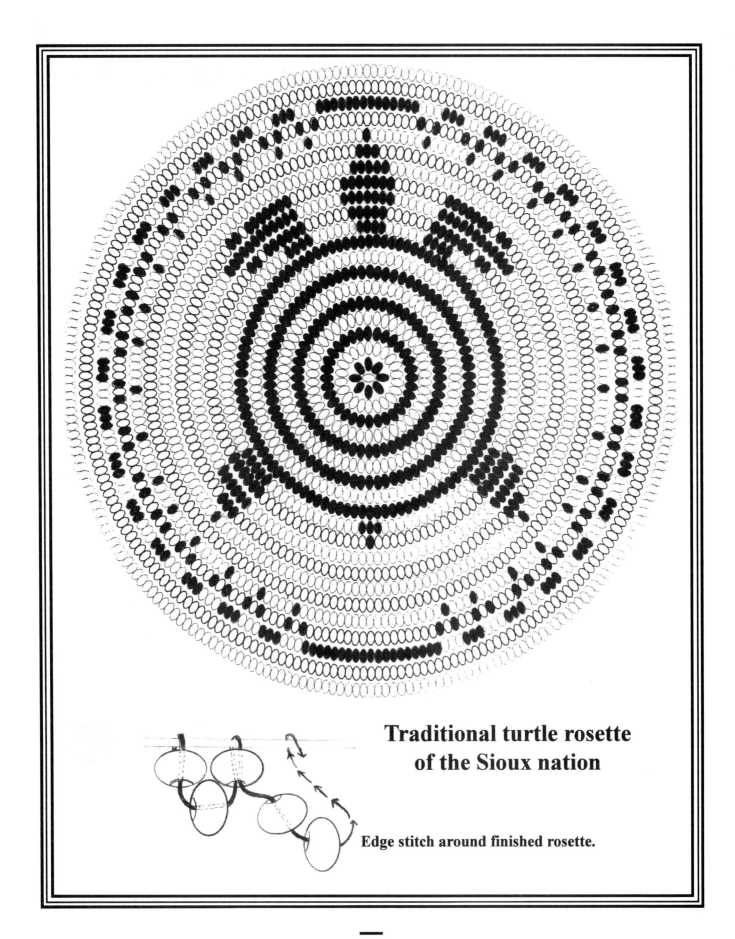

**Traditional turtle rosette
of the Sioux nation**

Edge stitch around finished rosette.

**Seneca Marsh Flower Basket Rosette
Pattern**

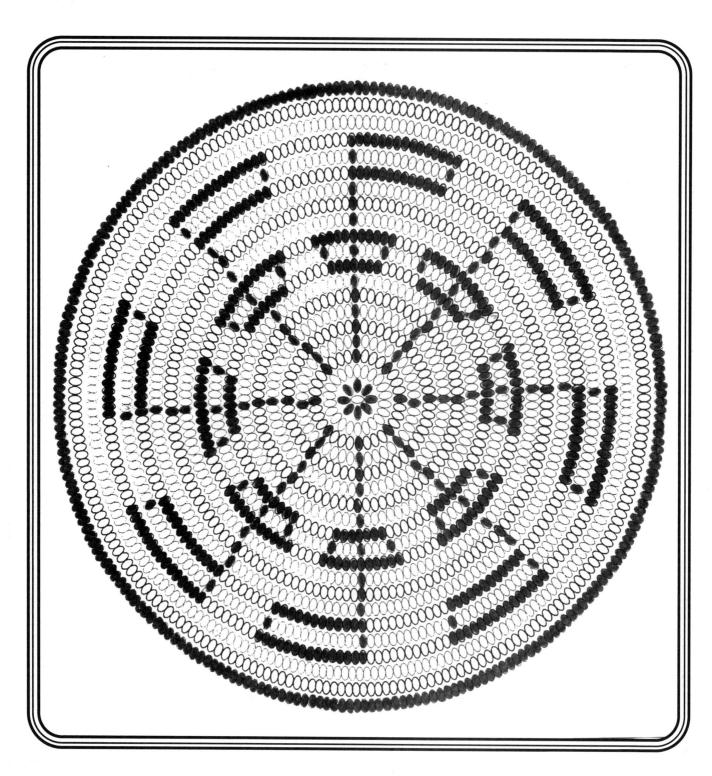

Cherokee Pin Wheel Basket Rosette Pattern

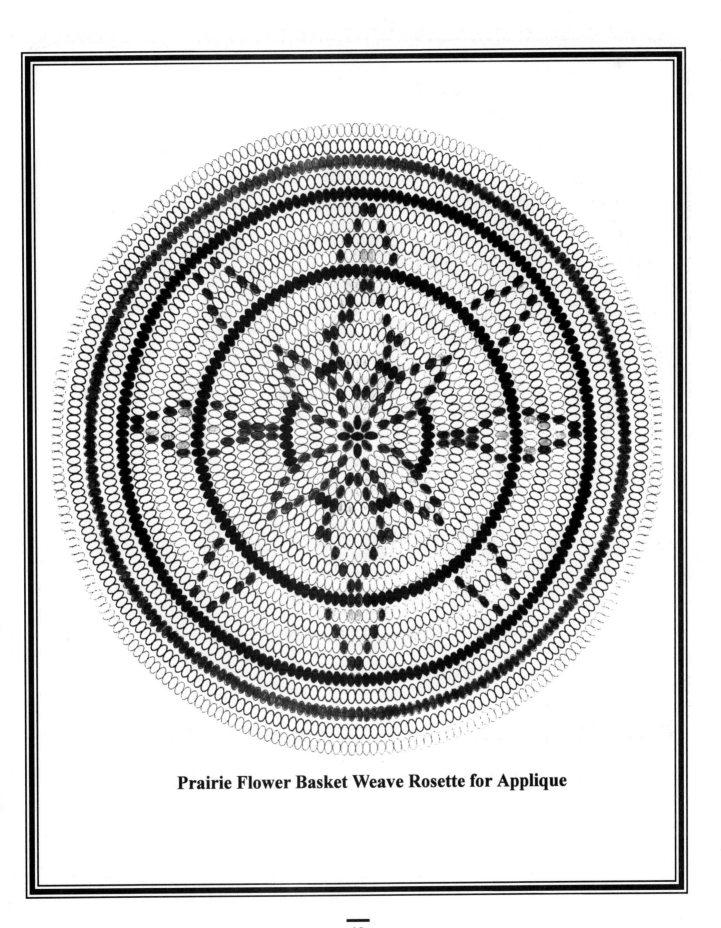

Prairie Flower Basket Weave Rosette for Applique

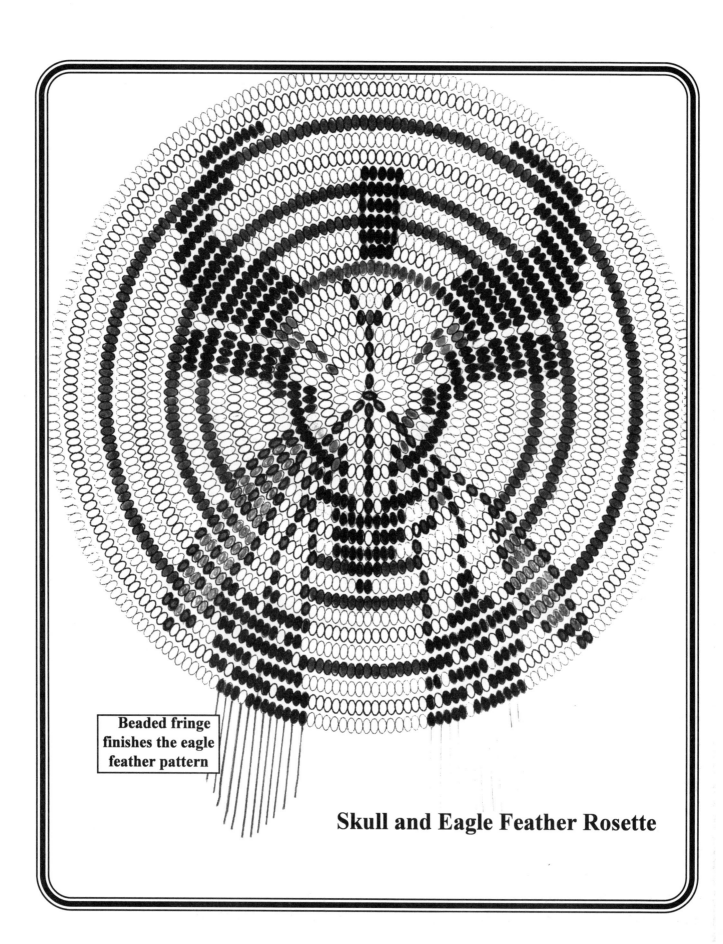

Beaded fringe finishes the eagle feather pattern

Skull and Eagle Feather Rosette

Crocheting With Beads is Fun!!

Crocheting with beads seems to be a technique everybody talks about but hardly ever uses. For some strange reason people put limits on what this technique can be used for. Most frequently I see it used for belts on ladies dresses. There are so many more areas this method can be used.

The peyote stitch is used in place of crocheting because it can be done on a round cord and is used for key chains, purse straps, headbands, belts, hatbands, bolo tie strings, necklaces, edging around garments, and much more.

Well think about this; crocheting with beads can do all that the peyote stitch can do and you only have to go through the bead one time with thread. Plus the crochet thread gives the beadwork a strong foundation to hold to and does not need the support of a rope or string through the middle of a crocheted rope to attach the beads. It forms it's own cord or fabric as you chain stitch the beads into place.

I am a collector of antique, beaded purses. Some are knitted with beads, some are appliqued with beads and some are crocheted with beads. A few of these purses are over one hundred and fifty years old. The oldest purse in my collection is two hundred plus years and is in good shape.

I told you all of that to get to this point; the technique used for the oldest purse is crocheting with beads, using the simple chain stitch illustrated in this chapter. I'm convinced that, when done right, this technique will endure as much wear as the peyote stitch.

One of the reasons bead people shy away from crocheting with beads is they think it to difficult to pre-string the beads onto the crochet thread. There are simple ways of doing what seems impossible. We will get into stringing the beads as the first step.

Before we get into describing the steps locate a cross stitch pattern that is rather short and simple or use one of the smaller, geometric, color graphed patterns in this volume.

Next, get all the beads together, in the colors needed for that pattern. Each color in its own separate container, flat enough to dip a needle into and come up with a bead without spilling all the other beads that you have already picked up off the needles end.

Sometimes you can get away with beads that are not uniform in size with this technique because, they do not lay tightly one against the other. Each bead has its own stitch, therefore it can move a little in its own space allowing the irregular beads to move into place. However, the old rule still holds true "Beads sized in uniform make for uniform sized beadwork".

Now for the threads. You will need a thread designed for beading, according to the size of your bead. For this technique I use the kevlar thread. It is almost unbreakable and is small enough to fit through the smallest beads. For the crochet thread, choose the size available that goes through the beads. If the crochet thread is to large and dose not fit through your beads then go to a heavy beading thread in place of it. A size D, Nymo thread works through size 11/o beads.

You will need a small size crochet hook. If you are using the Nymo size D thread, use a size 13 crochet hook. If you are using the crochet thread a size O crochet hook will do.

Now we get back to stringing the beads and reading the pattern.

Step #1.... Thread your beading needle with the kevlar or regular beading thread. **Do not cut the thread loose from the spool.**

Beginning at the top of the pattern, reading from **left to right**, top row, String all of that row of beads onto the beading thread. Next, from **right to left,** string all of the second pattern row of beads on to the beading thread. Continue stringing each row of the pattern in this fashion. Left to right, right to left until each row is strung onto the beading thread.

I use my dinning room table to lay the long string of beads out as they are strung. You can break the beading thread and begin where you left off as long as you don't loose count of the rows.

When you have strung all of the pattern rows on to the kevlar or beading thread, tie the end of the kevlar or beading thread to the end of the crochet thread, using a knot that will not slip. Do not use the crochet thread for looping the knot. Use the smaller thread you strung the beads on so the knot will be small enough to pass through the beads. Add a dab of nail polish to the knot and allow to dry.

Step #2... After the nail polish has dried, gently slip the beads from the beading thread onto the crochet thread. When all the beads are on the crochet thread, beginning at the bottom of the pattern wrap the strung beads on an empty paper towel center or roll them on a round stick.

Step #3... You have just completed the most difficult part of this technique. If you have not failed to string each bead in the pattern, you have only to master the chain stitch illustrated in the next pages to complete the project.

Go to the illustration for visual aid as the chain stitch is described.

Make a chain stitch without the bead to begin the chain. Push the first bead up against the chain stitch and hook a loop. Draw the next bead through the loop. Repeat the chain stitch with each bead.

When you have completed the first row, chain **two** loops without a bead. Hook the last bead chain stitch on the first row. Pull a loop without a bead. Pull a loop with a bead and push the bead through the loop.

Connect each stitch of the second row as you go, hooking the chain loop of the first row that lines up with that stitch, pull a loop. Pull a second loop and push the bead through the loop. Go the next chain etc......

Each row begins the same. Always chain two loops without a bead before starting the next row.

I know this seems very awkward, especially if you have never crocheted before, but if you practice on a small pattern you will soon catch on and be rewarded with the knowledge of a wonderful fast moving technique that can be use many different ways.

On the illustration page of this technique we show how to make a crocheted rope. This rope can take the place of any neckline on any beaded necklace or be worn as a necklace by itself.

For a color lined crystal effect in the beads, without taking a chance on the lined beads that sometimes fade, use a multi colored crochet thread through clear crystal seed beads. You will get a spiral of repeated colors showing through the beads, and only have to invest in one color seed bead.

I have used the colored thread technique mentioned above for the neckline of bolo strings. It compliments the cabochon rosette beadwork used as a bolo and adds a touch of class to a hatband.

Rather then use the traditional findings for the back of a bolo when used with crouched rope. I attach a small piece of elastic with a snap to hold the bolo on to the beaded rope. The elastic holds well and will not break beads or slip up and down the rope.

You can add fringes to the ends of the rope or use the rope as a base for a necklace and add fringes anywhere along the rope. Choker length allows you a collar base to hang a fringed pattern from.

These are only a few suggestions for the use of these beautiful ropes. I'm sure there are many more to experiment with.The illustration shows a four bead rope but it can be done with up to eight size 10/o beads and still hold it's round shape.

Chain stitch a 4 bead chain and connect the circle at the first bead

Connect circle in direction of arrow

Arrows indicate stitch placements

Make a chain loop with a bead between each bead as you progress around the circle.

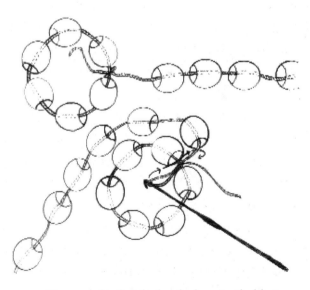

If you prefer that the beads do not spiral but lay one above the other, connect a string of six beads beads and chain a loop without a bead every other stitch., using the empty loop to connect to the circle each time.

Crocheting a Pattern With Beads

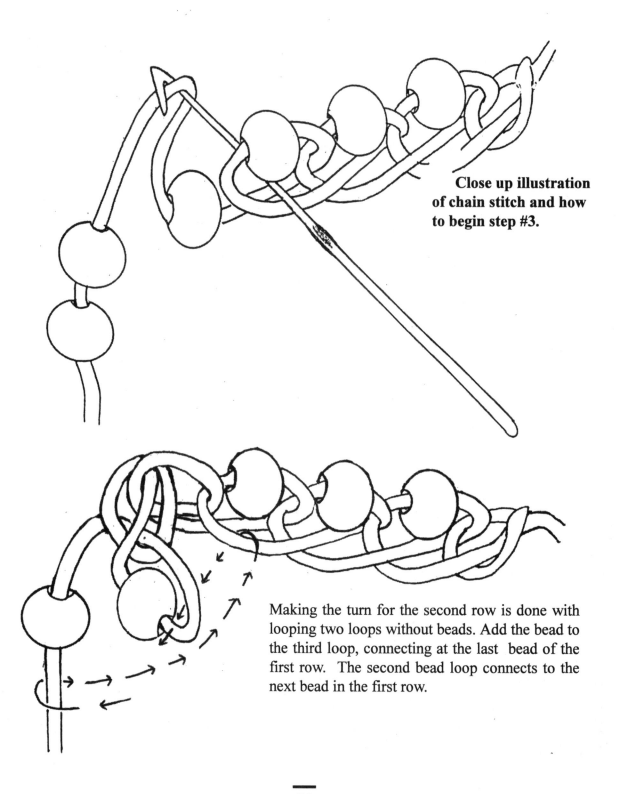

Close up illustration
of chain stitch and how
to begin step #3.

Making the turn for the second row is done with
looping two loops without beads. Add the bead to
the third loop, connecting at the last bead of the
first row. The second bead loop connects to the
next bead in the first row.

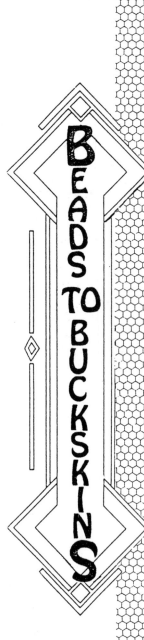

Doris Barnes surprised her husband with these beautiful appliqued tigers on a leather vest. Size 15/0 beads. Notice the horse hair whiskers.

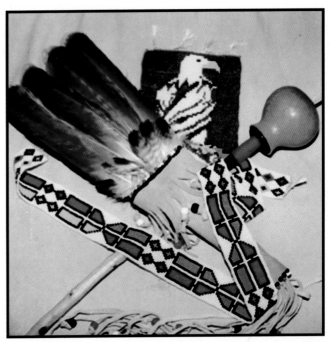

Michelle Wetzel of Moberly Mo., has loomed an eagle and a very colorful strip to accompany the traditional gourd rattle and fan with costume.

Judy Otero of a newly formed beading society in Albuquerque, N.M. has covered this acoma seed pot with size 11/0 beads, using an off loom technique. Wonderful accomplishment Judy, and good luck to all of you in your new venture at the Arts &Crafts Mart, Albq. N.M.

Jackie Bread has beaded a very colorful purse with an image of Plenty Coups in the pattern. Jackie expresses a wonderful talent for beading and I admire her arrangement. The pattern is from a Susan Hess design, Published by Jeanette Crews Designs, Inc."Portrait of Famous American Indians.

Designs by Jennifer Tallbear

The author has a very talented relative. Last year she sent Jennifer a large assortment of stone cabochons, pearls and beads and asked her to arrange them into jewelry. Jennifer's outstanding talent for design and color is quite apparent and greatly appreciated.

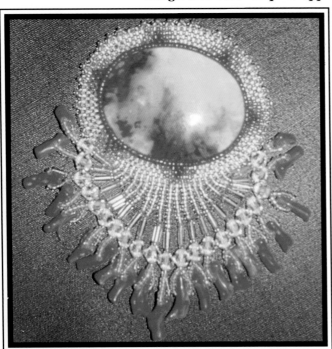

Rare Carri-Plume Agate cabochon. Fringed in red coral and crystal.

Mexican Crazy Lace Agate cabochons were used in this lovely brooch and earring trio. Size 14/o beads.

Wyoming Jade cabochons were used for this brooch and earring set. Gold and glass beads are surrounding the cabochon and in the fringe. Stunning--both by nature and craftsmanship!!!

The black jet beads enhance the design of this necklace and earring combination with a beautiful focal point of the Montana Agate cabochons.

58

Jennifer Tallbear Designs

circles of Rhodochrosite have been incorporated into this design. Jennifer has selected the rhodocrosite polished slices to enhance the beauty of this fan shaped beaded brooch with earrings. Trimmed with fresh water pearls.

The top set of cabochon earrings and brooch are Montana agate with soft pink, white and black beads. The dream catchers are of the same colors with a crystal glass heart trim.

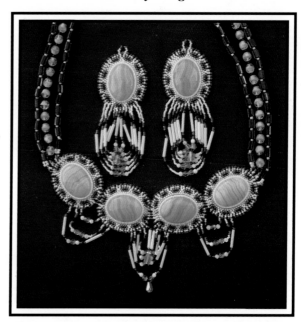

When this stone was named "Blue Lace" they must have had royalty in mind. Jennifer certainly reflects it in her arrangement of beads around the cabochon.

This lovely arrangement of Blue Lace cabochon in Necklace and earrings demands attention. Very elegant.

Lois McCoy, of Tandy Leather in Redding, Ca. has appliqued a very large beaded kachina. Bright, colorful ,and very well done Lois.

Nelson Begay is a Navajo, traditional, head man dancer known throughout the world.He has toured Europe and is well known in the U.S.A. He beaded this fan for the Author as a gift, years ago.

This pouch is a Navajo rug pattern in brilliant red, blue, yellow, and black on white leather. Made by Nata Natun of N. M. Size 15/o Hex beads on brain tanned leather.

Freida Bates has once again demonstrated her expertise in the field of loom beading. She calls this piece "Desert Nights". Notice the detail, shading and dimension of her work. Stunning!

Susan Cochran has created this striking black jean jacket with an African design. On the back, note the dimension in the face design, the lizard overhead and the butterfly design encompassing the collar.

In the front view of the jacket, Susan has again implemented the lizards with beetles on each lapel. Very attractive and unusual!!

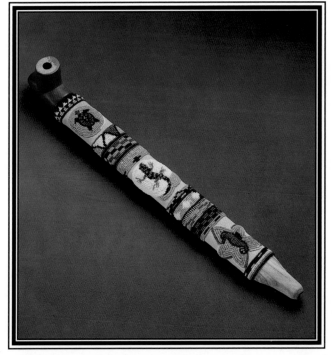

The pipe in the photograph is one Susan picked up at a pow wow. She said it wasn't very attractive, but bought it anyway. What an improvement she has made with this beaded design.

Susan has a great eye for the African bead design. Her talent shows in this leather purse. Extraordinary work and imagination, Susan!

Melody Abbott has appliqued this native face on a brown leather purse. The beadwork is completely done in brown, black, eggshell, and grey. Very unusual and yet excellent craftsmanship.

Melody has incorporated the antelope for background of this majestic warrior on purse front. Beads are size 14/o. Fringe and frame is done in matted bugles. Your art continues to impress myself and thousands more, Melody.

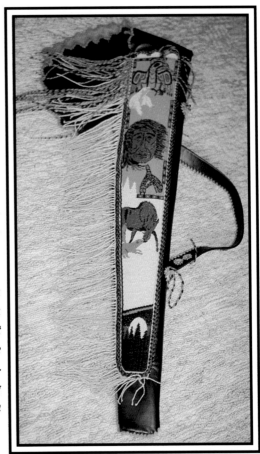

Melody has designed two gun scabbards. The left photograph has a buffalo, eagle, indian, and white wolf head incorporated into a beautiful pattern that graces the length of the scabbard.

The right photograph exhibits Melody's ability to transform a Northern look to her patterns. She has created a polar bear with totem design at the top. A breezy indian head with a symbolic claw, then a horse with wolf nipping at his nose. Notice at the bottom of the scabbard-- the moon gleaming through the evergreen trees.

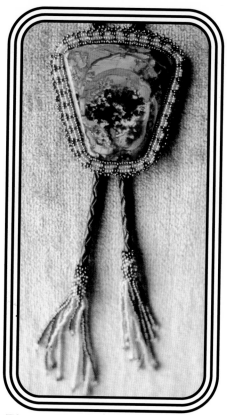

The author has created this bolo tie. The Morrisonite cabochon enriches this piece of beadwork for an extravagant look to enhance any man's wardrobe.

Author's design. The Rhodochrosite cabochon has been encompassed with white sz.14/o and pink sz.16/o beads to create a rose effect with an accent of green leaves. The fringe is finished in fresh water pearls.

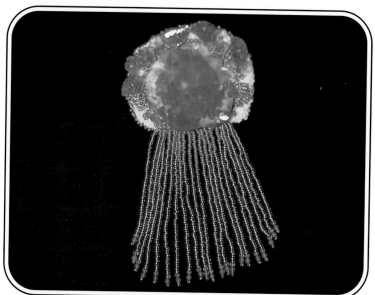

Amethyst crystal flowers with jade leaves arranged around a cluster of amethyst crystals ,gives a soft natural look to this piece.Created by Author. Hand carved flowers are from her private collection.

The author's sister-in-law, Doris Barnes has constructed these beautiful green paua shell broaches, bolo, and earrings with bronze twisted bugles. Beautiful!!

Margo Fields in Albq.N.M. designed this extremely unique necklace pouch with a twisted look on the neckline. A lovely one of a kind piece.

While in Gallup N.M. this year I stopped to see my friend Beverly Morgan at Windy Mesa Store. This beautiful ceremonial rosette was on display and she allowed me to share it with you. Sz.13/o cut beads form eagle feathers around the tepee.

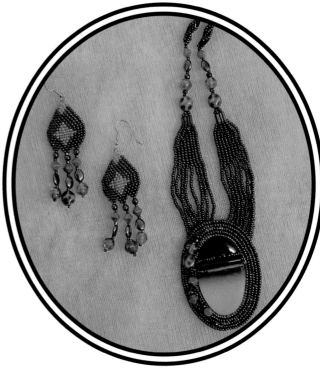

The contemporary design in this set of earrings and broach is one of Margo Fields wonderful arrangements . The cabochon rests at a slant.

Margo has used bronze around this cabochon with larger matching neckline and earring beads. The twisted neckline gives the effect of gold chain

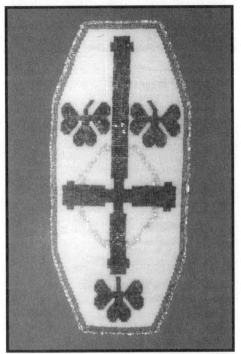

This Native Alaskan beadwork is done by Richard V. Howe, SR. in its bright red, blue, and green.

Richard teaches beading to" Order of the Arrow" (camping society with Boy Scout of America).

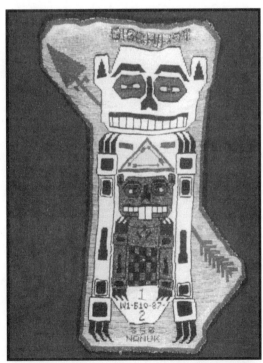

Richard Howe has chosen red, white and blue for this design. Great detail!

This unique design is done in red, white and blue. The beautiful statement has been incorporated with the intricacy of the beadwork. R. Howe

This pattern begins a chapter of dot to dot patterns designed to help you with the direction of beads and placement of needle for a more detailed finished piece. Each dot represents a needle placement. Between each dot, string proper amount of beads necessary for that stitch, depending on the size bead you are using.Pick up the beads that fill the stitch and pass the needle down through the material and up through the middle of the stitch. Go through the last half of the beads on that stitch again.(See plate # 7 for illustrated stitch). Now you are in position to pick up the beads for the next stitch and angle them in the direction of the next dot. We hope you enjoy this series of patterns. Drop us a line to the address on the back of the book. We appreciate your opinion, (no phone calls please).

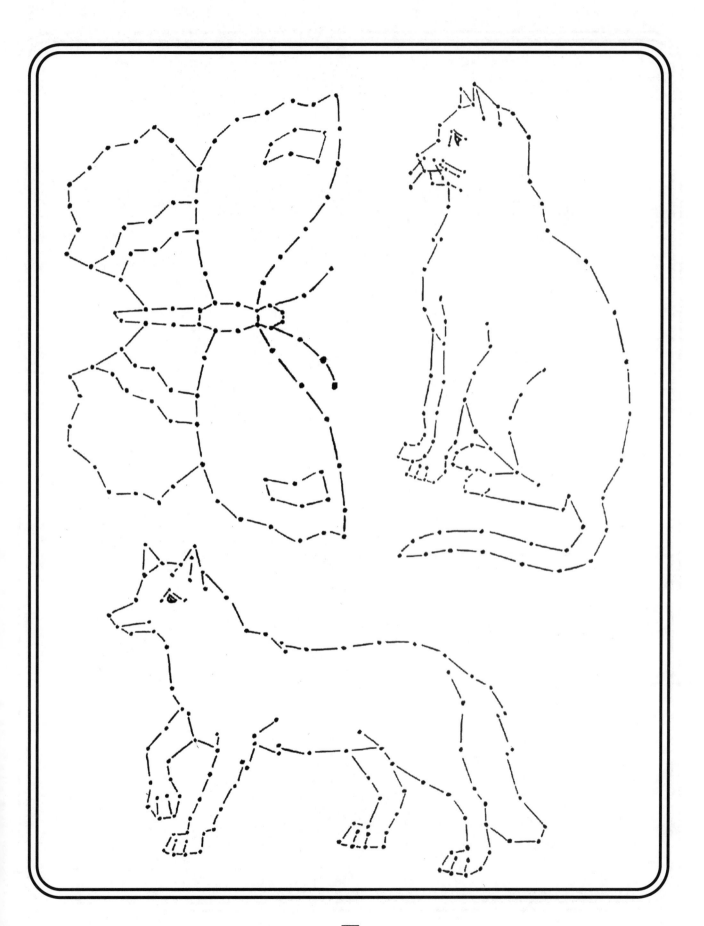

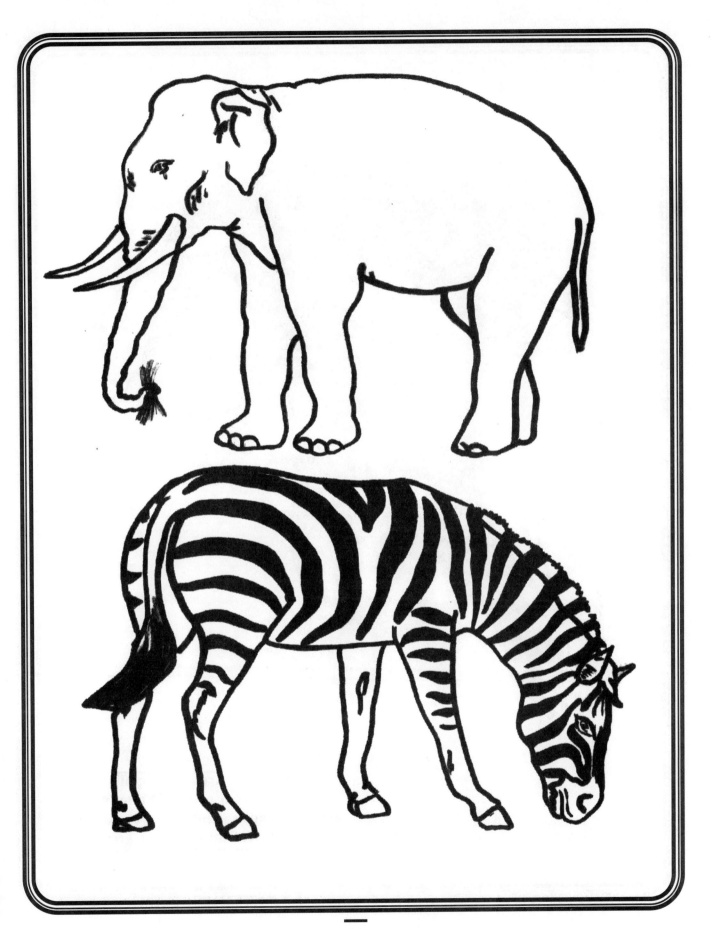

King of the Arctic, for applique technique. Suggested colors, White, medium blue for shadow depth and eyes, dark grey and light blue. Outline in dark grey.

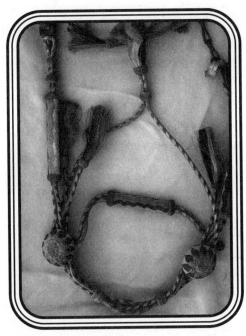

Those of you that admire craftsmanship that lasts forever, I'm sure will appreciate this ninety plus year old headstall and braided reins done in dyed horse hair by the inmates of a Wyoming prison at the turn of this century. The hair is still bright pink, yellow, green, red and white. These items are a gift, cherished by this Author, from her old friend "Russell Daud" of Gillette, Wy.

MICHELLE WETZEL created these beautiful, bright and colorful moccasins, fully beaded in red, black, blue and yellow on white leather.

DORIS BARNES has used her beading ability and unique craft ideas to create two sets of beautiful tigers. She has attached horse hair for whiskers and appliqued sets of three on the back and front yokes of his & her vests.

Margo Fields Creations

These beautifully designed necklace pouches were done by Margo Fields of Albuquerque, N.M. Margo has used an unusual twist beading technique on the necklines and fringes of these magnificent patterns. She displays a wonderful conception of what colors and shapes go well together.

Deb Horak of Odessa, Wa. has beaded these Historic figures using black and white beads, into a fur trimmed rosette, medallion necklace.

Deb Horak gets very colorful on the buckskin pouch and rosettes shown above. Yellow, red, orange, white and a splash of blue trimmed in black, reflects Native American Traditional.

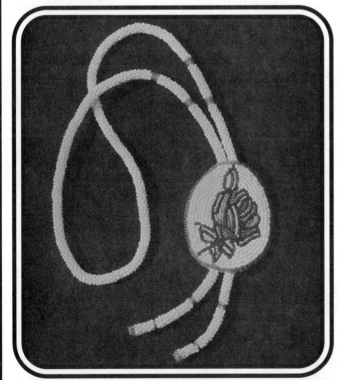

This lovely appliqued rose bolo was done by Deb also. She has used the peyote stitch on the neckline to compliment the rose.

The butterfly hair piece is appliqued in red, yellow, light and dark blue and the stick piece is peyote stitched with fringe through appliqued base. By Deb Horak.

Traditional Feather Fan of the Native American Indian

Creating a traditional feather fan is a fun project for people of all ages. Any type of feathers can be used as long as they are legal. Feathers from the birds of prey such as the eagle, hawk, owl or any other protected species are illegal, unless you have a permitted, release from the government to possess such feathers. Many of the Native American Indians are exempt because of their cultural, religious background in using the eagle and hawk feathers. I have never known of any N.A.I. to abuse or disrespect the feathers of such birds.

For the fan you will need the following materials. #1- Five large feathers and five small plume feathers. Turkey or pheasant feathers can be purchased at your local craft store. #2-One square foot of beading leather. #3- Leather glue and hot glue gun and glue sticks. #4- A wooden dowel, 1/3 inch by six inches long. #5- A male and female threaded aluminum dowel coupling. The female coupling will be placed in the handle and the male in the base of the fan, so the handle can be screwed off when packing for a pow wow. #6- If you are not going to bead the feather stems, you will need enough yarn or sinew to wrap each feather. #7-For the authentic fan, a small piece of rawhide was used to form the base that holds the feathers. If not authentic, a stiff plastic will do. (the plastic lid of a coffee can works well). In the illustrated pages of this chapter we show a wooden handle with the feathers arranged in it. If you have

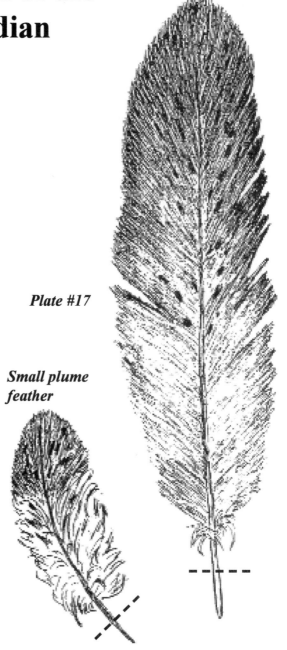

Plate #17

Small plume feather

Wrap the feathers from the plume to the point, in a thin strip of soft leather, applying glue as you wrap. Beading is optional, however it will be easier to bead the area between the plume and dotted line before you assemble the fan. Allow the glue to dry completely. Peyote stitch is the suggested technique. Traditionally the base of the feather was wrapped with a colorful sinew or thread.
Below the line will be glued into the handle .

access to the proper tools (a jig saw, sand paper and small drill) you can use this technique. #8- Beading and glover (leather) needles. #9- Seed beads and beading thread.

Before you begin your fan make sure the feathers are clean. If there is any dried skin left on the stems, soak the stems in cold water until the skin softens and peel or scrap it off. Any fleshy residue will attract insects that will eat the feathers. Gently wipe the feathered area using a soft cloth dampened with a mild disinfectant. Use an upward stroke to clean the feather. Do not go against the plume direction.

After you have cleaned the feathers and allowed them to dry. You can begin constructing the fan.

Step #1-Cut a strip of soft beading leather 1/8 in. wide by 4 in. long. (one strip for each feather). Do each large feather one at a time. Carefully apply leather glue to the stem of the feather, arrange a small plume feather in place to the stem of the larger feather. The plume of both feathers should be even. Lay the feathers on the edge of a table with the glued stem extending over the edge. If necessary place a light weight on the opposite end of the feathers and allow the glue to dry to a tacky consistency. Wash all glue from your fingers before picking up the feathers. Next wrap the leather strip around the glued area in a spiral. Trim off the excess leather at the bottom of the feather stem at a pointed angle. The small plume stem will not be as long as the larger feather. Allow the glue to dry completely.

Wrapping leather around the stem

of the five feathers not only reinforces the strength of the stem, but adds years of wear, plus gives you something to attach your beadwork to.

Step #2-If you are going to bead the stems of the five feathers, now would be the best time, before attaching the feathers to the base of the fan.

Measure the amount of stem that will remain above the base of the fan and bead only that area. The beaded area on each feather should vary slightly if you are using a staggered feather arrangement, as illustrated in plate #18-C below.

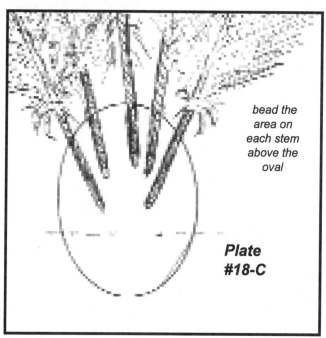

bead the area on each stem above the oval

Plate #18-C

The original fan feathers were wrapped with sinew or colorfully dyed quills of the porcupine, in place of beading. As the glass beads made their way across the continent they were added to the decor.

Certain stones were also incorporated into the decor of the fan. The Navajo use turquoise in a lot of their ceremonial fans, while many of the eastern tribes use shells and agate. However only certain people of high standing in the tribes were allowed to use stones that represented sacred religious meanings.

Step # 3-Cut two ovals of plastic from the plastic coffee can lid.(the actual size shown in plate #18-A). After you have beaded or wrapped the feathers with sinew, hot glue the un-beaded tips of the stems to one of the plastic ovals in the position illustrated in plate # 18-C. Do not glue below the dotted line illustrated on the plastic oval.

Step #4-Hot glue the second plastic oval, (down to the dotted line), to the back of the first oval, covering the feather stems.

Step #5- Lay the feather arrangement aside for now and prepare the wooden dowel for the handle. On the top end of the dowel file a groove across the center and 1/2 inch deep. Illustrated step #5, plate #18-B. Place a piece of tape around the dowel at the base of the filed groove for support.

Step #6- If you plan to have a disconnecting handle, carefully cut the dowel into, **one inch** below the groove. Next (using a cement glue), glue the washer on the cut end of the dowel opposite the groove and the blunt screw, to the other piece of dowel on the cut end. If you want fringe hanging from the bottom of the handle, glue the fringes around the handle now.

Step #7- Now you are ready to assemble the top of the fan to the base. Hold both pieces of the unglued plastic ovals together and slip them into the grooved dowel. Hot glue around the groove to hold the plastic permanently. Next, separately glue and wrap both pieces of the dowel with leather, covering the edge of the screw on one and

the edge of the washer on the other. The fringe ends should be covered and the plastic base up to the beadwork on the feathers. Allow the leather wrapped pieces to dry completely.

Now that you have completed the body of your fan the fun of beading the handle and fan base begins.

Most tribes of the Native American have certain colors that represent their clan or nation and the men use these colors on their ceremonial garments. However the women are prone to wearing beaded flowers and soft geometric designs. So unless you are going traditional, bead a design that pleases you.

The peyote stitch works best when covering a long round object. The peyote can be extended or reduced to the measurements as you go.Volume three of this series teaches two versions of the peyote stitch.

For the wooden handle fan illustrated below use the same technique for beading and wrapping the feathers. However you will have to drill the holes for the feather stems in the top. The inset washer and screw are also glued into drilled holes. The

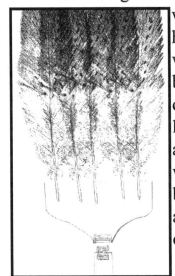

wooden base and handle is covered with leather, then beaded. The feathers on this fan are usually spread evenly across, and the beadwork is done in-between the feathers also, making it a fan of beauty.

Five Feather Fan

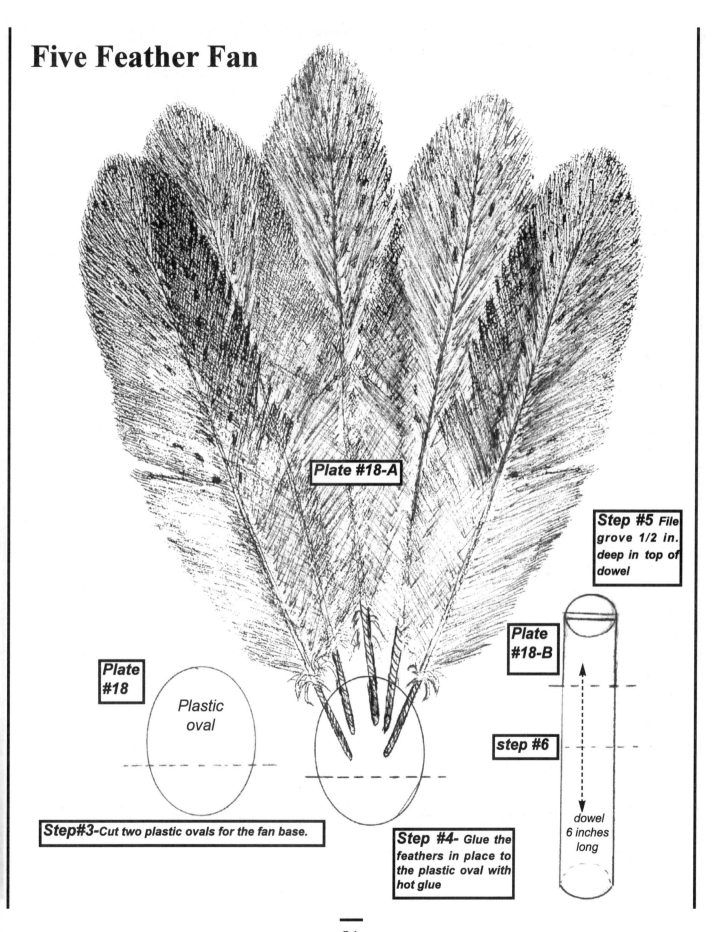

Plate #18-A

Step #5 *File grove 1/2 in. deep in top of dowel*

Plate #18-B

step #6

dowel 6 inches long

Plate #18

Plastic oval

Step#3- *Cut two plastic ovals for the fan base.*

Step #4- *Glue the feathers in place to the plastic oval with hot glue*

Equestrian pattern above for loom or off loom Geometric techniques.
Horse head oval for appliqued belt buckle, hair piece or patch.

William Tohee of Carney, Ks. has created this vibrant colored appliqued blanket. He has chosen red, yellow, green, purple, lavender, orange, and blue on this dark background. Beautiful!

The Author's sister-in-law, Doris Barnes would be sure to enchant even the most avid animal lover with her alluring tigers. These have been appliqued onto a black leather vest. The detail on these pieces is incredible!!Notice the horse hair whiskers of the cat.

In this photograph, we show the craftsmanship of William's work. He is very accomplished in finger weaving belts and sashes. He also restores antique beadwork to its original state.

Doris appliqued two beautiful matching white tiger for the front lapels of her black leather vest. In this issue we show another set of gold tigers done by doris for her husband,Everett

While in Quartzsite Az. this year the author purchased the little median earrings on the left done with brickstitch and looped fringe she made the indian princess pair with black braids and clasped hands. using the off loom tech. in vol.#3.

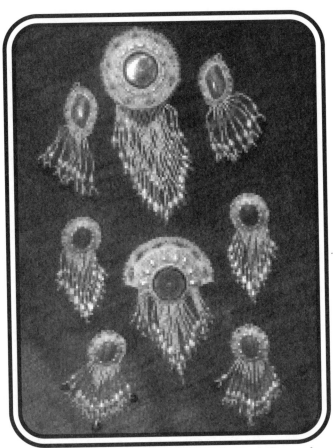

Jennifer Tallbear- Rosette brooch (top) & earring (technique ill. this issue) Fan shown in color pg.

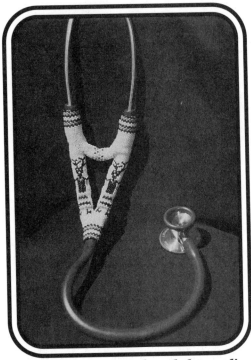

Lela Holcomb has remembered the medical people in her creation with this very cute idea of peyote stitched, southwestern design on a stethoscope. Bead colors used, white, blue and black .

Frieda Bates has a very talented daughter "Antoinette Marie Rutheford" designed and created the White dentalium shell and brown leather, fringed Chokers. Nice arrangement!!!!

Through out this series I have mentioned my Navajo mother and shared with the readers what a great lady she is. Heneretta Bedonie has been an inspiration to me and I have illustrated this pattern as a tribute to her with love. She has shared all she has with those in need, and cared for those who needed care.

Navajo Geometric Patterns for Loom

Horned Owl

**Graphed for loom, off loom, embroidery or cross-stitching
with beads**

Related Volumes of The Beads to Buckskins Series

Look for these related volumes at your local craft store or book store. They can also be obtained direct from the publisher.Each volume will always be available.

<u>Volume One</u>: If you are a beginner, you can learn "Native American Indian techniques" the easy way with over 180 easy to follow patterns both graphed and freehand. Also included; loom beading, the peyote stitch, overlay and applique stitch, the lane or (lazy) stitch, five edge or fret stitching techniques, loom beading without a loom, the brick stitch, daisy chain, geometric designs and patterns, plus a beautiful color section.

<u>Volume Two</u>: Has over 200 patterns including a moccasin and buckskin shirt pattern with unusual looming techniques. Included in this volume: split loomed necklace instructions, secrets revealed in beading, spanish lace earrings, silhouettes, cradleboard earring, chevron chain, indian flower, peyote stitch overlay or applique stitch. Eight pages of full color photograph section.

<u>Volume Three</u>: Shows some prize winning beadwork in the color section, as well as instructions and patterns of how to do it. The loom beading without a loom technique has been illustrated to show how to complete a split loom necklace without the use of a loom. Another feature in Volume Three, is how to bead with stone cabochon incorporated with seed beads to make a beautiful and unusual piece of jewelry. You will learn how to make a squaw dress with moccasin pattern instructions, brain tanning techniques, beaded fringe, and instructions for beaded buckles. A revised and simplified peyote stitch is also included.

<u>Volume Four</u>: In this volume, we introduce an exciting style of beadwork that can be applied to any cross stitch pattern or design. Inlaying beadwork into leather, embroidery with beads, and a helpful hints from the author on business-minded crafters are also included.

<u>Volume Five</u>: In keeping with the demand for new, creative ideas in beading, this volume exposes many time saving short cuts. Each with easy to follow, step by step illustrated instructions. We introduce new techniques in beading and reveal many short cuts and best kept secrets of beading. And of course, there are new and exciting loom patterns and techniques with illustrated instructions. We teach crocheting with beads and advanced crocheting using beads with lots of new, creative earring fashions.

<u>Volume Six</u>: Volume Six completes the first half of this series. Each volume teaches beadwork and Native American Indian Media, as well as beading fashions of other countries. In Volume 6, we look at designs in tribal identity and its meaning. Quilling and Tambour beading techniques with illustrations are presented as well as, off-loom weaving methods and a new concept on beading. You will enjoy the color sections and new patterns exposed.

<u>Volume Seven</u>: This volume delves into beadwork patterns and techniques for the nineties through the twenty-first century. Illustrated techniques for cutting your beading time has been revealed, plus new earring techniques for cutting your beading time has been revealed, plus new earring techniques and patterns. We give tips for marketing your crafts. Also included: Southwestern history, transposing pictures to bead graph, the lacy daisy weave, conchos, conchos and bead braiding, bead braiding necklaces, double needle cross over, cross needle earring, contemporary bead weaving, beaded boot spats and much more.

<u>Volume Eight</u>: This volume focuses on cradleboards, their construction and beadwork. Featuring full color photographs of antique cradleboards and newly constructed ones. Illustrated also are the side stitch weave (two versions), beaded boot tabs, beaded buckskin flowers, beaded button cover, beaded hair bun cover, peyote stitched necklace pouch, garment decor with beads and a special eight pages of color patterns.

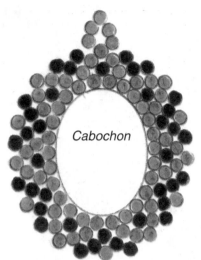

Cabochon

Brickstitch Patterns
Strips for Cabochon

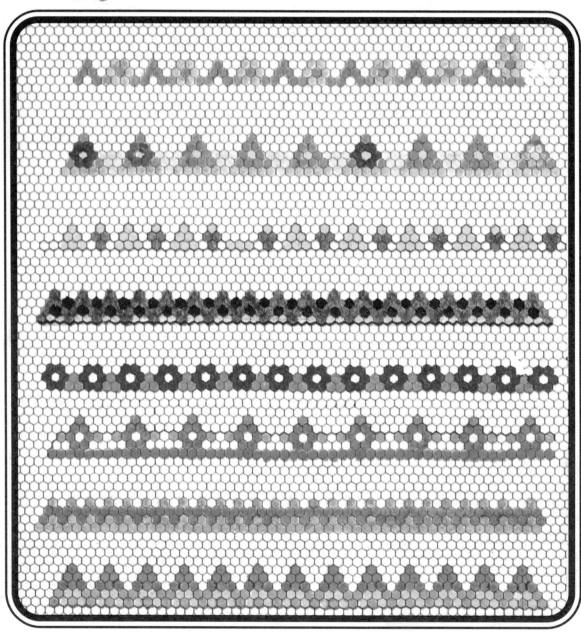

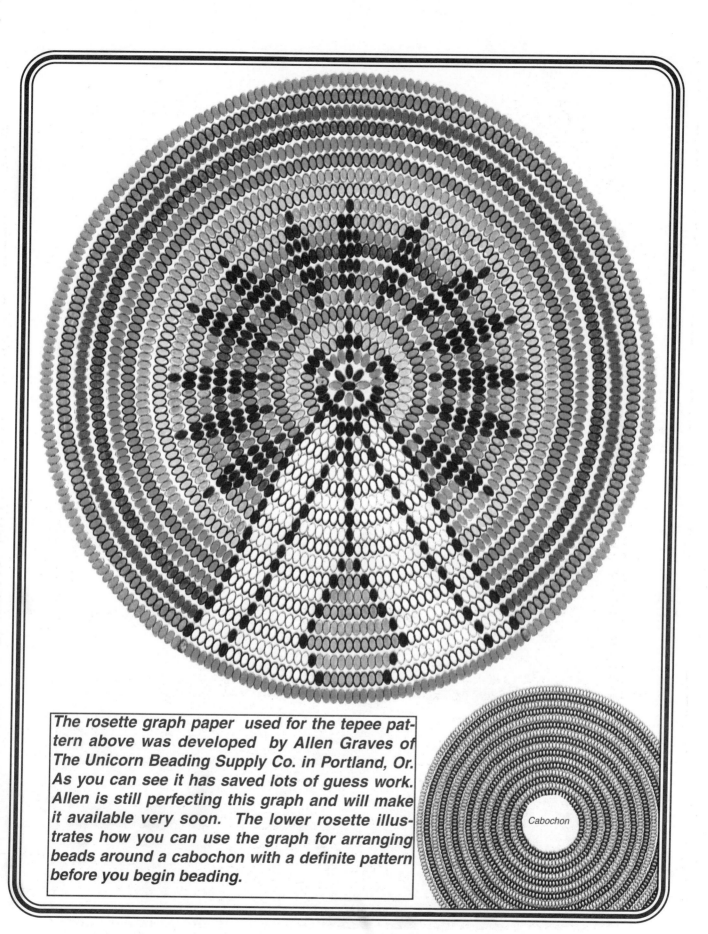

The rosette graph paper used for the tepee pattern above was developed by Allen Graves of The Unicorn Beading Supply Co. in Portland, Or. As you can see it has saved lots of guess work. Allen is still perfecting this graph and will make it available very soon. The lower rosette illustrates how you can use the graph for arranging beads around a cabochon with a definite pattern before you begin beading.

Cabochon

Peregrine Falcon and Masked Filcher Water Bird. For Applique Technique.

Duck in Flight for Applique with beads

Nez Perce Warrior

Each animal head or the indian warrior can be a separate pattern.